MEDIEVAL
MAPS

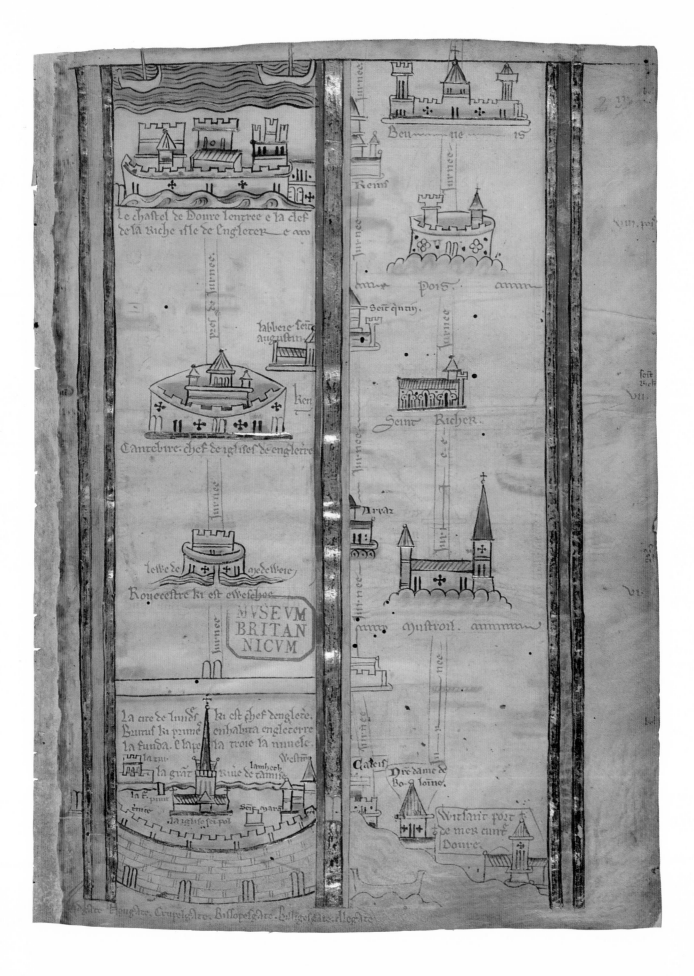

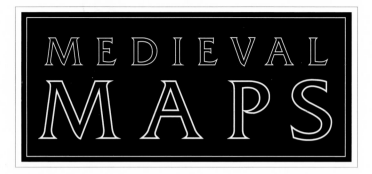

MEDIEVAL MAPS

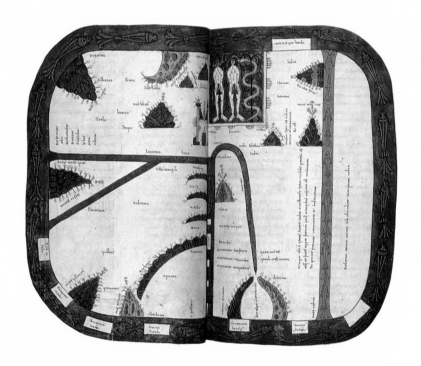

P.D.A. HARVEY

UNIVERSITY OF TORONTO PRESS
TORONTO AND BUFFALO

© P.D.A.Harvey
First published 1991 by
The British Library Board
Great Russell Street
London WC1B 3DG

Published in North America by
University of Toronto Press 1991

Canadian Cataloguing in
Publication Data

Harvey, P. D. A.
  Medieval Maps
ISBN 0-8020-2806-3
1. Cartography — History.
  2. Maps, Early.
I. Title

Designed and typeset on Ventura
by Roger Davies.
Colour origination by York House
Graphics, Hanwell
Printed in England by Jolly and
Barber, Rugby

Frontispiece

1 Itinerary by Matthew Paris

Few medieval people used or understood maps, and this itinerary, set out in graphic form by Matthew Paris, monk at St Albans, in the mid-thirteenth century, was a highly original work. On this first of its five pages, 35 by 25 centimetres, the left-hand strip shows the road from London (bottom left), with its city walls and the medieval St Paul's Cathedral, to Dover (top left), with its castle. Crossing the English Channel, marked by waves and boats, the right-hand strip gives alternative routes from Calais and Boulogne (bottom right) to Reims and Beauvais (top right).
British Library, Royal MS. 14 C.VII, f.2

Half-title illustration
See fig. 17

Title-page illustration
See fig. 39

Acknowledgments

I am grateful to Mr Tony Campbell and Dr Peter Barber, both of the British Library's Map Library, for very kindly reading a draft of my text and for helpful comment and discussion which have significantly improved both text and illustrations; also to Mr Roger Davies, the book's designer, and Mr David Way, who initiated and supervised its publication, for their skilful, sympathetic and efficient help throughout my part in its preparation.

For permission to reproduce maps in their possession, thanks are due to the following:
Cambridge; the Master and Fellows of Corpus Christi College (18)
Cambridge: the Master and Fellows of Trinity College (10)
Dijon: Archives Départementales de la Côte d'Or (77)
Ebstorf: Kloster Ebstorf (13,21,23)
Hereford: the Dean and Chapter (22,24,25)
London: the British Library Board (1,3,4,6,8,14,15,17,19,20,27,28,29,31,33,34, 36,37,38,39,40,41,42,45,46,47,48,49,50,51, 52,55,56,57,58,60,62,63,64,65,66,67,69,71, 72,73,75,76)
London: the Trustees of the British Museum (70)
London: Public Record Office (68)
Munich: Bayerische Staatsbibliothek (16)
Nancy: Bibliothèque Municipale (43)
New Haven: Yale University Library (44)
Oxford: Bodleian Library (59,61)
Paris: Bibliothèque Nationale (30)
Rome: Biblioteca Apostolica Vaticana (35,53)
Rome: Museo Capitolino (7)
St Gall: Stiftsbibliothek (9)
Venice: Biblioteca Nazionale Marciana (54)
Vienna: Historisches Museum der Stadt Wien (74)
Vienna: Österreichische Nationalbibliothek (2)

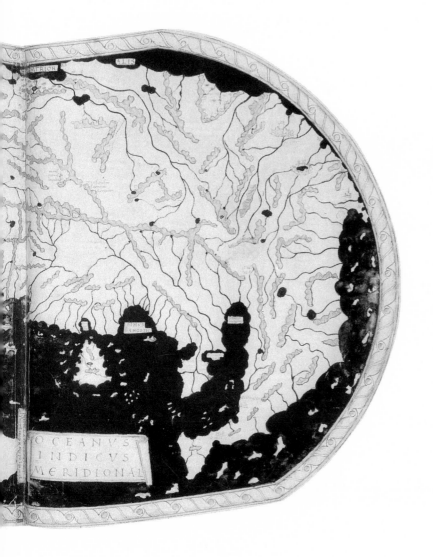

Contents

Verullo · Annamaria

VIII · Bottus · VIII · Sonita · XII · pirenis · XI · luntulis · VII · Iouia · X · Sirotis · X · Solentio · IX

A Quadrata · XIII · Padfines · XV · Sisela · Burnomilia · XII

HADRR CABHAVRE · XII · Aserie · O

XIII · Hedino · Sardona · N · XI

R · XII · XII

Polentia · Sacrata · VI · Aulor fl · Tinna · Castello furnani · XII · Lupu maritima

Plausulas · XIII · firmo viceno · X · fisternas · III · Cirulos · VII · Pitinum · XII · Pif

Adaquas · IX · Surpicano · XV · interverto · Aque cutilie · VIII · Reite · XVI · AdNouas · XVIII · Cirto · VIII · fidenis

AdMartis · von · Palernuf · III · forveri · XII · VII · Acquo faltico · XVI · fanfat · Adponte · IIII

Intermarana · XII · Aqua uiua · VII · Advicesimu · X · Adrubris · VI · fonte Adriani

Adfine Recine · VI · Interannio · VI · VI · Adfertiu · via clodia · III

Fugitui · VIIII · veros · VI · Bobiana · Iorio · XII · via Aurelia

VIII · careias · VIII · turres · VIII

meum · VI · Pyrgos · X · Alsium · VI · VIII

Gallum Gallinarium

Clucar · XVI · Thuburbiminus · III · Tinnaria · XV · ciodas · XVIII

Cuifidrio · IIII · Sicilbba · V · Inuca · II · Admercurium · III · Adpertu · XVIII

Callis · VI · veris · Aurta · X · Tuburbomaius · XV · Vhellaria · XV

Risca · XVIII · seggo · Anula · Aurpfibam · VII · VII

Thafarto · Atualartho · thuges

CHAPTER ONE

Introduction

Maps were practically unknown in the middle ages. This may seem an absurd way to begin a book that displays a whole pageantry of maps from many different parts of medieval Europe — but it is a fact, and it is one we must accept if we are to appreciate what these maps were, what they set out to do, how they appeared to the age that produced them. We are apt to take maps of every sort for granted, from the small-scale general map we use to find where places are to the roughly sketched plan we draw to give someone directions or for some other purpose. So far were people in the middle ages from our awareness of maps today that there was no word meaning map either in the languages of everyday use or in the Latin used by the Church and for learned writing. When contemporaries referred to what we would call a map they would use some word meaning either diagram or picture, and this was indeed how they must have viewed them: they were pictures of landscape, of regions or of continents, or they were diagrams setting out spatial relationships in graphic form just as they might set out other relationships — administrative, philosophical, theological.

Nearly all the maps drawn in the middle ages were more akin to the sketch map produced for a particular occasion than to the general map that we consult as a work of reference. Each was drawn for strictly limited purposes, with one class of user in mind — the Mediterranean navigator, the long-distance traveller by land, the law-court judging a dispute, the educated person seeking instruction in distant lands and customs. What it showed and how it showed it depended on what purpose it was to serve. Today, travelling by car, we may use a strip map of a fast motor road; it shows us clearly and accurately the junctions and exits, the service stations and the distance from one to another. But it cannot help us to find our way across country once we leave the particular road for this is not what it was designed for. If we are to understand and assess a medieval map we must find out why it was drawn, what it was meant to do. Once we have done this — and it is not always easy to discover — we usually find that the map serves its intended purpose with fair efficiency.

It is because they are single-purpose maps of this sort, not maps for general reference, that many medieval maps look so odd to us. Certainly we shall go badly astray if we try to assess them as if they were all-purpose general maps, as if it was only limitations of technique that prevented medieval map-makers from drawing the geographical outlines we are familiar with today. Limitations of technique there certainly were; but there were even more profound limitations of concept. Most medieval maps fall within well defined groups or traditions of map-making. If any other sort of map was drawn we ought to see it as an imaginative leap of real originality. It simply did not occur to people in the middle ages to use maps, to see landscape or the world in a cartographic way.

Instead they often produced written descriptions where we would be more likely to draw a map. Rather than plans of fields there would be what

2 Peutinger table
This medieval copy preserves an otherwise lost map of the fourth century — a diagrammatic road map of the whole Roman empire, set out on a strip nearly 7 metres long and 34 centimetres wide. In this section the central band is part of Italy with Rome and Ostia on the right. Below it is Spain and above are parts of central Europe and the Balkans. Along the top is the Danube, with a town marked at Budapest ('Aquinco'). Not intended as a general map, it is a detailed and accurate guide to routes.
Vienna, Nationalbibliothek, Codex 324

3 Survey of fields without a map

There survive many medieval written surveys which, without the aid of a map, set out in intricate detail the arable strips or other pieces of land belonging to a particular village or manor. This page is from an early-fifteenth-century English example, describing lands at Portchester in Hampshire

British Library, Additional MS. 70506, f.184v

are called terriers, describing often many hundreds of individually owned plots and strips one after the other (**3**). For journeys there would be itineraries, listing the successive places along the route. Not many of these itineraries survive — probably most were written on scraps of parchment or paper and thrown away once the journey was over — but those we have are of great interest. Among them are the list of churches that Archbishop Sigeric of Canterbury visited in Rome when he went there to receive the pallium in 990 and the route he followed on his way home (**4**). Another is the elaborate fourteenth-century itinerary which gives routes from Bruges across most of Europe with distances in local measures — leagues in France, miles in Germany, day's journeys in Hungary and so on. Another was drawn up at Titchfield Abbey in Hampshire between 1405 and 1408, listing routes to other houses of the Premonstratensian Order in England. But it needed the imaginative genius of Matthew Paris, thirteenth-century monk at St Albans, to convert the written itinerary into a strip map, setting out graphically the route from London to Rome with thumbnail sketches of the places on the way (**1**).

When people in the middle ages did draw maps it was thus something quite unusual, something alien to their normal way of thinking. There were of course more medieval maps than those that survive, for many must have

4 Itinerary of Archbishop Sigeric
Travellers in the early middle ages never had maps to guide them, but sometimes had written itineraries, lists of places along the routes they were to follow. Even these itineraries are scarce. In this eleventh-century manuscript a Latin list of the churches at Rome visited by Archbishop Sigeric of Canterbury in 990 is followed by a list of the places ('submansiones') where he stopped on his way back to the English Channel.
British Library, Cotton MS. Tiberius B.V, f.23v

disappeared in the course of time. But from chance references to maps now lost and from some other indications we can be fairly sure that the maps we have reflect accurately the overall pattern of medieval cartography: the survivors belong to the same groups, were the same sorts of map, as those that have been lost. This leaves us with some difficult questions. How did the maps that were drawn in the middle ages come into being? Where did the idea for a map come from? How was it compiled? Some of the most sophisticated maps of the middle ages had no obvious antecedents, drew on no pre-existing tradition; their authors are anonymous and we know nothing of how they were produced. The earliest sea-charts of the Mediterranean, the grid-map of Palestine, the Gough map of Britain, the scale-plan of Vienna — these, we shall see, are only a few examples of the medieval maps whose origins are wholly mysterious.

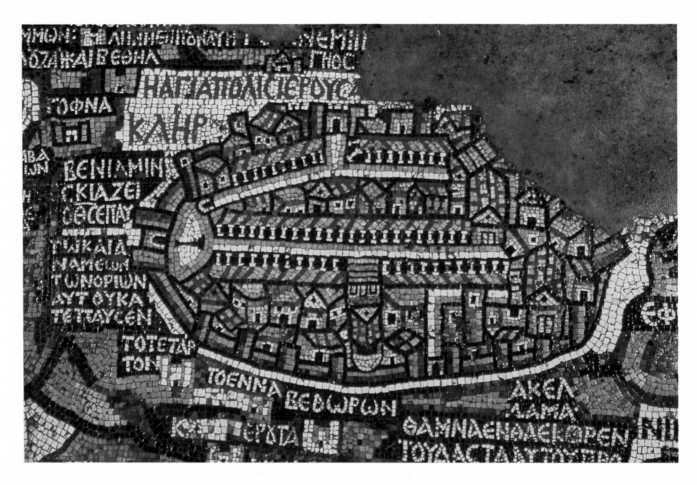

5 Madaba mosaic
At Madaba in Jordan are fragments of a sixth-century mosaic picture-map of the Near East. Originally it probably measured some 6 by 24 metres overall. This small portion shows Jerusalem with colonnaded streets, churches and houses.
Madaba

6 Roman surveyors' manual
Treatises by Roman surveyors of the first to fourth centuries AD were still being copied in the middle ages, but the surveyors' ability to draw scale-maps had long been lost. On this page of a twelfth-century volume of extracts from their works the upper diagram shows the two base-lines of the rectangular systems of fields laid out by the surveyors — the *decumanus maximus* ('DM') from east to west and *kardo maximus* ('KM') from north to south.
British Library, Additional MS. 47679, f.71

One problem hard to resolve is how far medieval maps drew on classical models. Medieval Europe was a society that functioned largely without maps, but the same was not true of Imperial Rome. The Romans seem to have been much more accustomed to maps of every sort than people in the middle ages were. We have quite a number of Roman picture-maps. Outstanding is the mosaic at Madaba in Jordan, a picture-map of Palestine including a view of the walls and colonnaded streets of Jerusalem (5), but there are others in mosaics, in manuscripts and even on an enamelled cup and painted on a shield. More impressively, Roman land surveyors used maps in their craft, which medieval surveyors did not, and their maps were drawn to scale, the hall-mark of a real understanding of cartography. But besides maps of surveyed fields we have plans of buildings carved on tombs, all drawn to scale, and fragments of a large-scale plan of the whole of Rome, carved on stone early in the third century AD and set up on a public building where it covered a wall some 13 by 18 metres (7). These show that maps — even the use of scale — were widely understood in the late Roman period; they were not restricted to particular crafts or to groups of officials. The same is probably true of the geographic maps, scale-maps of the known world and its various lands and regions; no examples survive from the Roman period, but we know them through medieval maps which we are confident were copied or derived from them.

Itam si in decumanū quartū lapidē posuerim̄. sequenti loco cen
turic quartuſ zamtuin uocabitur. Quod si numeruſ ipsi—is
scribitur ad summā. omīs clusateſ anguloſ centuriarum
lineis diagonalibus comprehe--deⁿ---ıs.

Sic & in toto fiet.
& gerioreſ anguli
centuriaſ claudut.
ab inscriptione
decumanↄ 11 ma
ximi. & cardi
niſ maxı oſ ı.

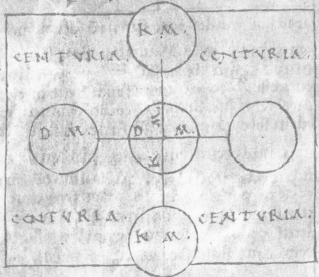

Cuoſ centuriaſ omīſ in se certiſ lapidib; geminauerimuſ.
illaſ que r. p. assignabuntur. quauiſ limitib; hereant
priuata terminatione circuibimuſ. & in pascua publica
siue in Siluas siue in utrāq; quatenuſ fuerint inscriptione
replebım̄. & ut in forma loci latitudinē rarior litterarū
dispositio demonstret. harum siluarum extremitates
per omes ang---loſ termı----abı⸝⸝⸝ıs.

		SILVA & PASCVA				
		PVBLICA AVLENSIV.				

Eadē ratione terminabım̄ fundoſ exceptoſ siue concessoſ.
& in forma sic loca publica inscriptionib; demonstrabimuſ.

11

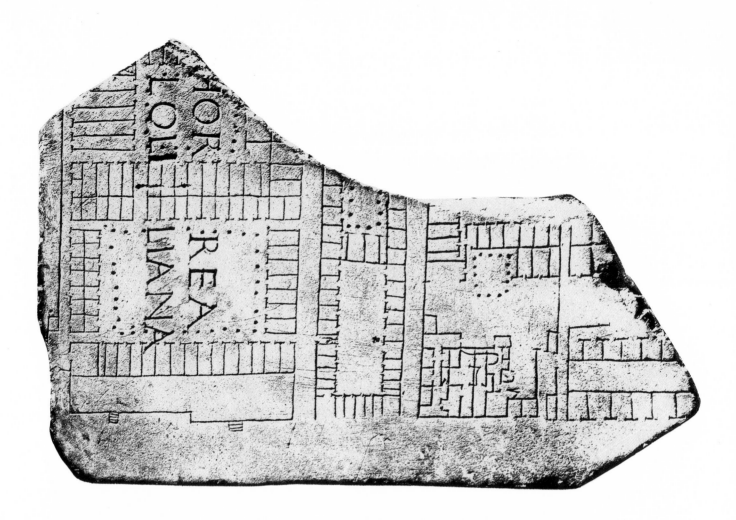

7 Carved plan of Rome
Only fragments survive of this
masterpiece of Roman map-making: a
plan of the city of Rome on the scale of
1:240, showing all buildings in outline
ground-plan. Carved in AD 203-11 on 151
stone tablets, it measured 13 by 18 metres
and covered the wall of a public building.
Rome, Museo Capitolino

These certainly were not the only Roman maps known to the middle
ages. The diagrams and picture-maps that illustrated Roman surveyors'
manuals were still being copied into late medieval manuscripts of these
texts (6). One great monument of Roman cartography we know only
through what seems to be a faithful copy drawn in the eleventh or twelfth
century; this is the Peutinger table, named after its sixteenth-century owner,
a diagram-map showing roads, towns and staging-points for travel
throughout the Roman Empire (2). But though much of the cartography of
the Roman period was accessible to the middle ages it was only in particular
instances or in limited ways that any continuing tradition can be traced.
Whatever medieval cartography may have owed to Rome, it certainly did
not take over the whole legacy of the classical past to continue to build on
this basis: much Roman cartography was lost for a long period or for ever.

We see this in the scale-plans of buildings. Arculf, a bishop from Gaul
who visited the Holy Land in 670, while on his way home was carried off
course to western Scotland. Here he wrote an account of his journey for
Abbot Adamnan of Iona, illustrating his text with plans of the Church of
the Holy Sepulchre and three other buildings; they are drawn in just the
same style as the carved plans of buildings or of the whole city that we have
from Imperial Rome, and we may surmise that in the original manuscript

— we have only late copies — they were drawn strictly to scale (8). We have one later plan that follows the style and conventions of the Roman surveyors: the extraordinary ideal plan for a monastery, with all its outbuildings, that was drawn probably at Reichenau, near Constance, in the early ninth century and sent to Gozbert, abbot of St Gall, where it is still preserved in the monastic library (9). But there the tradition ends. A twelfth-century plan of Canterbury Cathedral and its priory may well owe its inspiration to the St Gall plan (10). We can reasonably suppose that there were occasional contacts between the two monasteries in the early middle ages, no other plan of a monastery is known before the fifteenth century and some of the inscriptions identifying the buildings and rooms at Canterbury oddly echo those from St Gall. But there is no trace of the Roman surveyors in the Canterbury plan; their techniques and conventions have wholly disappeared, and it was not until the fifteenth century that ground plans drawn to scale reappeared in Europe. They then owed nothing to Roman precedent.

However, medieval map-makers may have drawn ideas from other sources besides the maps of the Romans. Europe was not entirely insulated from the Islamic world, which had cartographic traditions and styles of its own (11). These in turn owed something to Roman mapping and perhaps

8 Plan of the church of the Holy Sepulchre at Jerusalem

The four ground-plans of buildings that accompany Arculf's account of his visit to the Holy Land show traces of the conventions found in Roman surveyors' scale-plans. Arculf's journey was in 670; surviving manuscripts are all much later and this copy dates from the fourteenth century, long after the technique of drawing plans to scale had been forgotten.
British Library, Additional MS. 22635, f.44

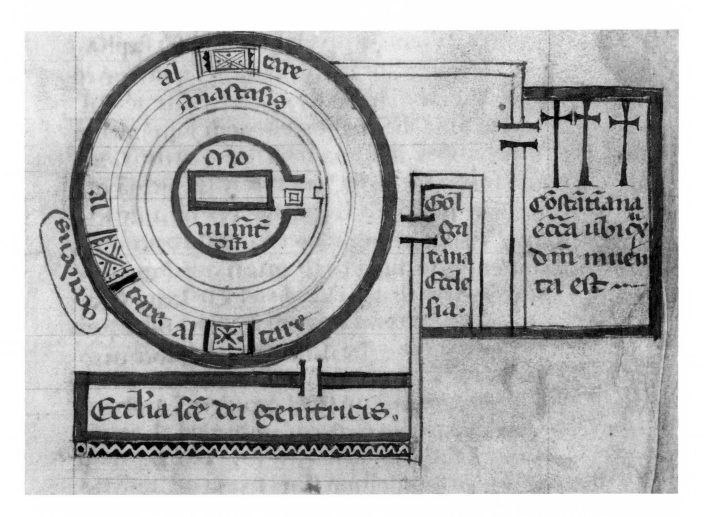

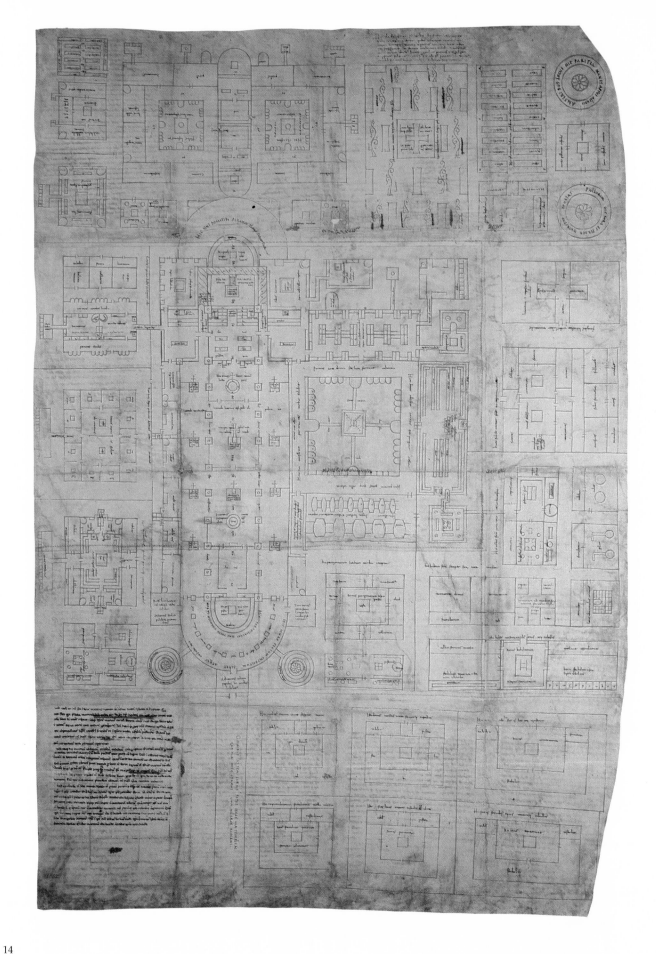

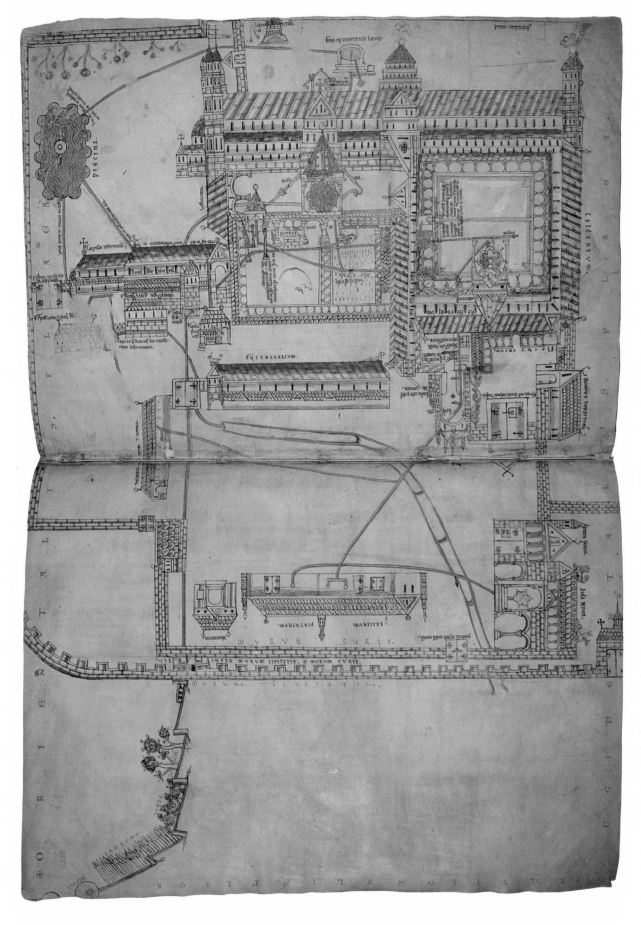

9 Plan of a monastery from St Gall

This plan was drawn probably at
Reichenau and was sent to the abbey of St
Gall, where it has remained ever since, as
a present to Gozbert, abbot from 816 to
837. It presents a model layout for a
monastery, with its church, cloister, living
quarters and outbuildings, all identified
— the physician's house, the coopers' and
turners' workshop, the houses for the
servants, horses and oxen, and so on. The
two double circles in the top right corner
are houses or pens for chickens and geese,
with their custodians' house between
them. Drawn on a grid, it is the latest
known plan in the tradition of the Roman
surveyors.
St Gall, Stiftsbibliothek, Codex 1092

**10 Plan of Canterbury Cathedral
and its priory**

The earliest known local map from
England, this plan of Canterbury
Cathedral with its monastic buildings was
drawn probably in the 1150s. Its purpose
was to show the improvements made
under Prior Wibert, in particular his new
water system, marked by the green and
red lines. Latin inscriptions identify the
buildings and other features, including
even 'The window through which the
dishes are passed for washing up'.
Cambridge, Trinity College, MS. R.17.1, ff.284v-285

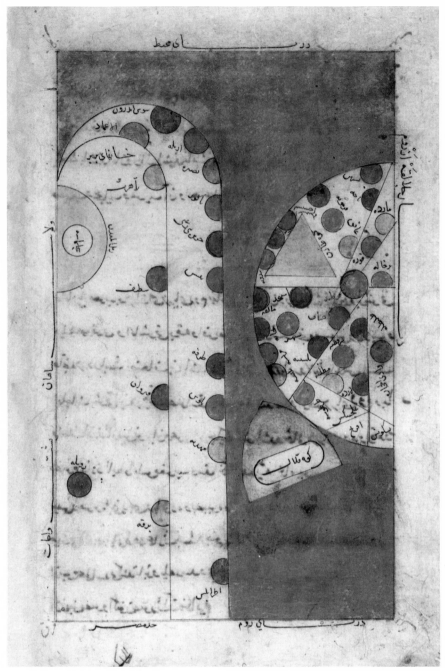

**11 Islamic map of the western
Mediterranean**

This page from a Persian copy of a
tenth-century atlas is typical of Arab
mapping. West is at the top; on the left
is north-west Africa, on the right
southern Spain. The coloured circles are
towns.
India Office Library, The British Library

right

12 Carved map of China

Carved on stone in 1137, this is a late
survivor of a Chinese tradition of
drawing maps to scale which went back
to the work of the cartographer Phei
Hsiu in the second century AD. Each
square of the grid is 100 li, about 50
kilometres. Even Chinese cartography,
at several removes, may have had some
influence on map-making in medieval
Europe.
Changan

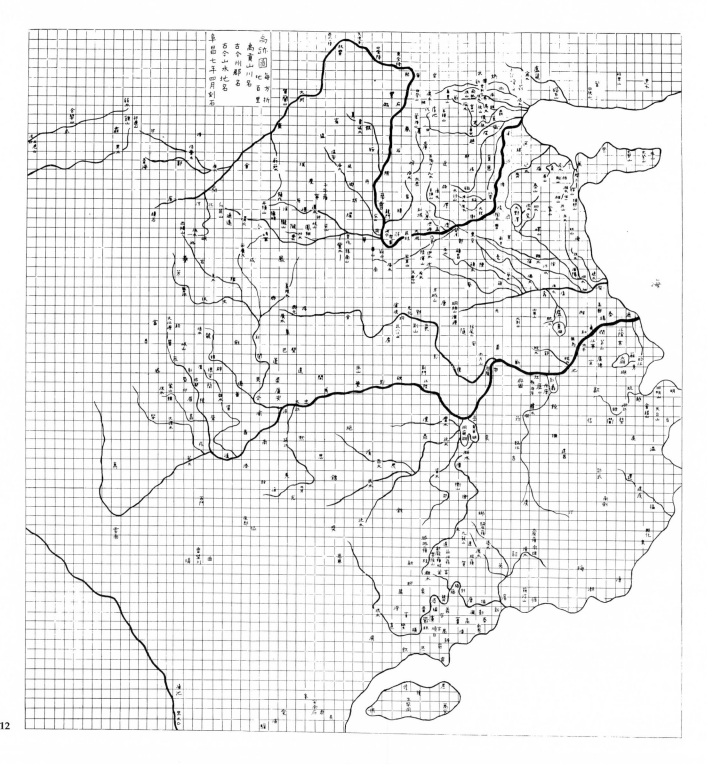

also to maps from China. The Chinese had developed the idea and the technique of mapping to scale by the third century AD and among other maps one of the whole of China, carved on stone in 1137, shows that the skills had not been forgotten by the time of Europe's middle ages (12). We know so little of the origins of many medieval maps that we cannot rule out the possibility of any influence, however remote.

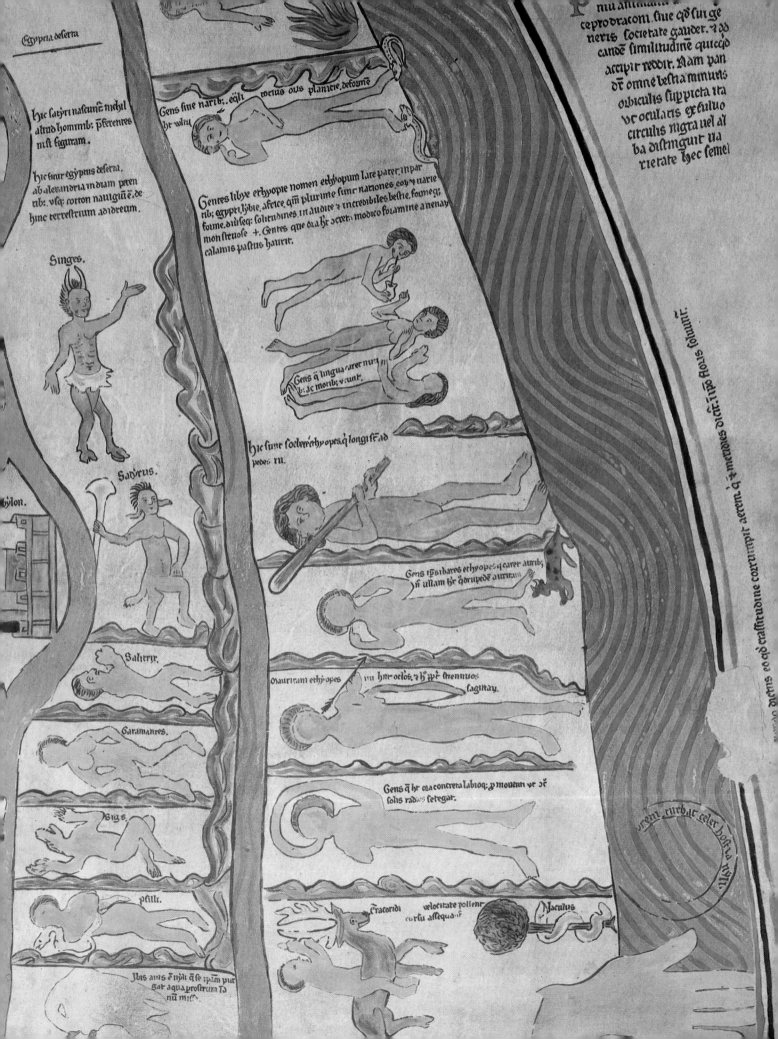

Egypta deserta

Hic satyri nascunt nichil aliud hominib; pferentes nisi figuram.

Hic sunt egyptus deserta ab alexandria in diam peren tib; usqꝫ cotton nauigiũ; de hinc terrestrium ad idreum.

Gens sine narib; eqli ht uultu

ctius ous planicie defoune

Gentres libye erthyopie nomen ethyopum late patet. in par tib; egypti, libie, africe, qm plurime sunt nationes. eoꝰ ꝗ uarie forme, diuseqꝫ solitudines. in audite z incredibiles bestie, formeqꝫ monstruose +. Gentes que ora hr actem modico foramine a nenay calamis pastus haurit.

Singes.

Gens ꝗ lingua caret nut ib; de morib; ueunt.

Sadrus.

Hic sunt foebere' ethyopes. ꝗ longi st ad pedes iii.

bylon.

Salitrix.

Gens ipsibares ethyopes ꝗ carer aurib; si ullam hr ꝗdrupede auritam

Garamantes.

Maurirani ethyopes iiii hr oclos. z h' ꝙ' triennuos sagittat

Sigs.

Gens ꝗ hr ora concreta labioqꝫ ꝗ mouenn ut ꝙ solis radns setegat.

Psilli.

Dracoridi velocitate pollent curtu assequant

Naculus

Ibis auis ꝫ nn̄ ꝗ se ipm pur gat aqua prostrum ta nu mic.

niu aiaium ceproꝺraconi. siue ꝗꝺ sui ge neris societate gauder. z ad cauꝺe similitudinē quicꝗꝺ accipit reꝺꝺit. Nam pan dr omne uestia minutis obiculis suppicta ita ut oculatis ex fuluo circulis nigra uel al ba distinguit ua rietate hec semel

que ꝺicitur typo floris soluunt

orient. turbat celer boria inflat.

CHAPTER TWO

World maps before 1400

13 Africa on the Ebstorf world map
The most elaborate world maps of the
thirteenth and fourteenth centuries were
used to convey a great miscellany of
information, not strictly geographical. In
Africa (the river on the left is the Nile) the
Ebstorf map describes many strange races,
among them people without tongues who
communicated by signs, people without
nostrils and people with four eyes who
were wonderful archers.
Ebstorf, Kloster Ebstorf

It is only in maps of the world that we can clearly see a continuous
tradition linking Roman and medieval maps. They were the only kind
of map that was drawn at all commonly in the middle ages, and well
over a thousand survive from the seventh century onwards, far more than
all other medieval maps put together. It is not surprising that the word for
map in English and in some other languages derives from the phrase used
for a world map in the middle ages: *mappa mundi*. But this did not mean
'map ot the world' — the idea of a map was only starting to take shape —
but 'cloth of the world':some world maps were painted on cloth as wall-
hangings and the phrase came to be more widely applied, first to world
maps in general, then to other maps as well.

Indeed, the vast majority of medieval world maps are scarcely maps at
all. They are diagrams — diagrams of the world — and are best understood
as an open framework where all kinds of information might be placed in
the relevant spatial position, not unlike a chronicle or narrative in which
information would be arranged chronologically. This information might be
of many different kinds. Certainly it included geographical information,
and in the fifteenth century this came increasingly to dominate these *mappae
mundi*, turning them into the sort of world maps we are familiar with today.
But in the earlier world maps the geographical element was only one of
many: the map was a vehicle for conveying every kind of information —
zoological, anthropological, moral, theological, historical.

Moreover, many of these world maps, from all periods of the middle
ages, provide just the framework with little if anything added — simple
diagrams, often no more than a few centimetres across, drawn as illustrations to philosophical or scientific treatises. Before the fifteenth century
nearly all world maps derive from one or other of two basic diagrams, more
or less elaborated. Both show the world as a circle. One has north at the top
and is divided by horizontal lines into seven bands, representing frigid,
temperate and torrid zones north and south of the central ocean river — the
zonal or climatic map (**14**). The other has east at the top and is divided by a
T-shape into the three continents, Asia at the top, Europe on the left and
Africa on the right — the T-O or tripartite map (**15**). A variant of this is the
quadripartite map, which adds a further continent, the Antipodes, on the
right, separated by the ocean river from Asia and Africa. Even such large
and complicated productions as the thirteenth-century Ebstorf and Hereford maps may both derive ultimately from the tripartite map.

Though less elaborate than these thirteenth-century maps, some much
earlier world maps presented far more than the basic diagram — indeed, it
would be wrong to see any general progression from the simple to the
detailed. Lambert of Saint-Omer wrote his encyclopaedia in the early
twelfth century, but the map that illustrates the various surviving copies of
the work derives from the then still popular book that Martianus Capella
wrote at Carthage in the early fifth century, the *Marriage of Mercury and
Philology*; in effect this was also an encyclopaedia, expounding in turn each

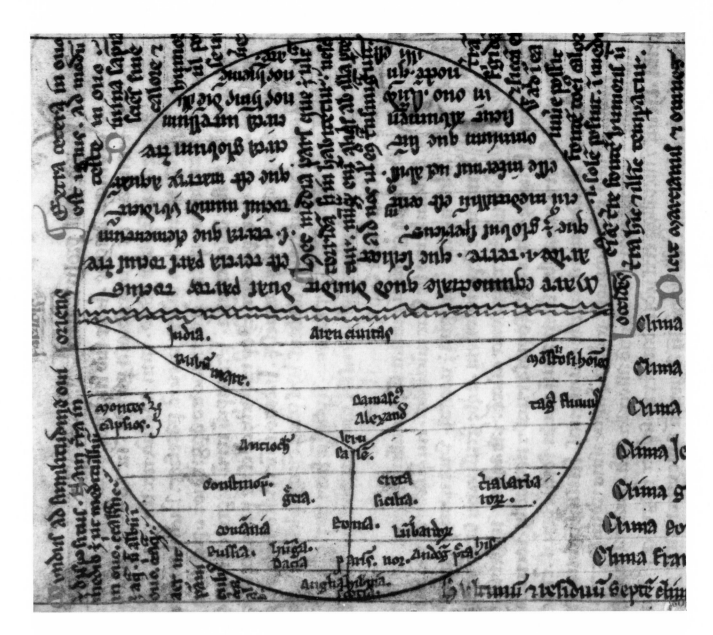

14 Zonal world map

This thirteenth-century world map,
though only 8 centimetres across, is more
than a simple diagram. The southern
(upper) hemisphere is filled with
geographical notes — when we have
summer they have winter, when we have
daylight they have night. The northern
hemisphere, separated from it by the
Equinoctial Sea, is divided into three
continents with Jerusalem at the centre
and also into seven zones, with the names
of a few lands, peoples and geographical
features appropriately placed.
British Library, Cotton MS. Julius D.VII, f.46

of the seven liberal arts, presented as bridesmaids at the wedding. The map
shows, schematically, some rivers and mountains as well as islands in the
ocean, and names the regions of Europe, Asia and Africa, while in the
Antipodes it places a paragraph of descriptive text. Most of the many copies
of another encyclopaedia, written by Isidore, bishop of Seville in the early
seventh century, are illustrated with a more or less simple T-O map; but this
may be elaborated to show mountains, rivers and cities, and islands not only
in the ocean but in the Mediterranean as well (16). The Beatus maps are an
interesting early group, so called because they occur in manuscripts of the
commentary on the Apocalypse written by the Spanish theologian Beatus
of Liebana in the late eighth century (17). Mostly four-sided, not circular in
shape, these Beatus maps illustrate the work of the apostles in spreading
the Gospel, and particularly prominent is the picture of Adam, Eve and the
serpent that marks the earthly paradise.

All these maps — like most medieval world maps — are built up from the starting-point of one or other of the simple outline world diagrams. The Anglo-Saxon or Cotton map is something quite different (19). It dates from the tenth or eleventh century and was drawn in England; its English origin is betrayed by the name it gives the Bretons, 'Suðbryttas', spelled with one of the runic letters used in England for *th*, but is anyway indicated by its location in a volume of Anglo-Saxon writings that belonged in the seventeenth century to Sir Robert Cotton. It was not, however, compiled in Anglo-Saxon England. Rather it is a copy, perhaps not a very good copy but the clearest we have, of a world map which must have been constructed in the Roman period and which probably contributed much to the geographical elements in many medieval world maps. It may even be that we have here a direct descendant of the world map which Marcus Vipsanius Agrippa, son-in-law of Augustus, compiled at the end of the first century BC and which was probably based on the survey of the world ordered in 44 BC by Julius Caesar. But whatever its origin, the Cotton map is extraordinarily important, and its significance, how far it is related to other medieval maps, has probably not been fully explored.

That there was such a relationship, that other medieval world maps drew on some version of the Roman map that lies behind the Cotton map, seems fairly certain. Some of its basic shapes — the Mediterranean islands, the

15 Diagrammatic world map
The simplest medieval map of the world was the T-O map: a circle divided by a T into the three continents of Asia, Europe and Africa. It is found in many copies of two works written in the early seventh century by Isidore, bishop of Seville: the *Etymologies* and *The Nature of Things*. This example is from an eleventh-century copy of the *Etymologies*.
British Library, Royal MS. 6 C.I, f.108v

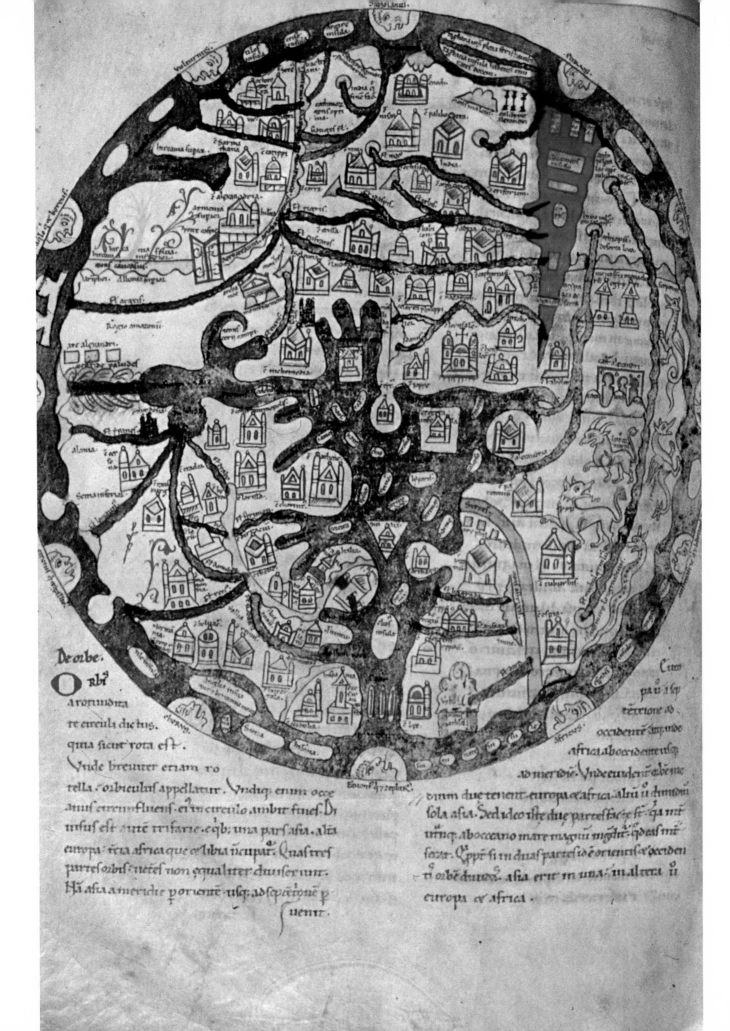

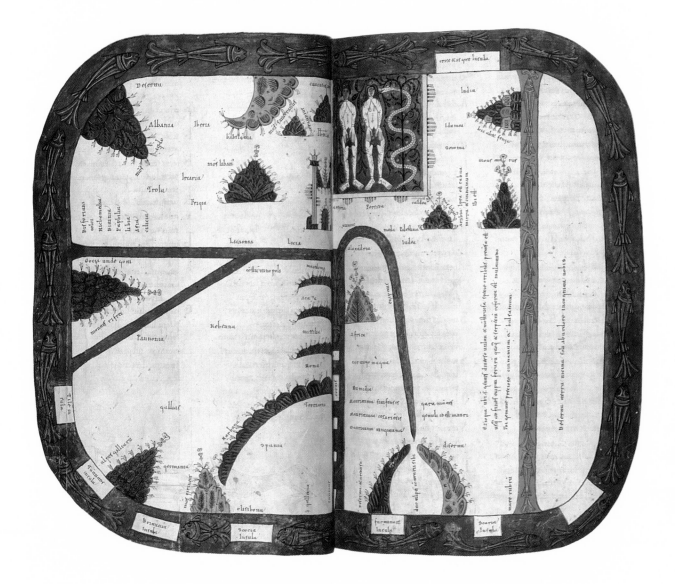

16 Isidore world map

Many copies of the seventh-century encyclopaedic works by
Isidore, Bishop of Seville, contain a simple diagrammatic world
map. This eleventh-century manuscript has a more elaborate
version, 26 centimetres across. The map is dominated by the
Mediterranean with its islands, among them the triangular
Sicily. In Europe, lower left, serrated bands mark the Pyrenees,
the Alps and the Apennines. The wedge-shaped Red Sea
appears top right.

Munich, Bayerische Staatsbibliothek, Clm 10058, f.154v

17 Beatus world map

Beatus of Liebana wrote his commentary on the Apocalypse in
eighth-century Spain. Surviving copies are illustrated with a
world map and this double-page example is from a manuscript
of the early twelfth century. The vertical blue line in the centre is
the Mediterranean, its continuation bending round to the right
is the River Nile and the vertical red line is the Red Sea. Two
rectangular islands (bottom left) are named Britain and
Scotland. At the top is the Garden of Eden with Adam, Eve and
the serpent.

British Library, Additional MS.11695, ff.39v-40

18   Henry of Mainz world map

This twelfth-century world map is the earliest of a related group, all with English associations, that includes the Ebstorf and Hereford maps. It illustrates a version by Henry, canon of Mainz Cathedral, of an earlier world chronicle, but the only known copy comes from Sawley Abbey, Yorkshire. At the foot of the map is Spain, with Ireland and Britain shown as long irregular islands to its left. The tower with two turrets, prominent towards the top of the map, is the Tower of Babel.

Cambridge, Corpus Christi College, MS. 66, p.2

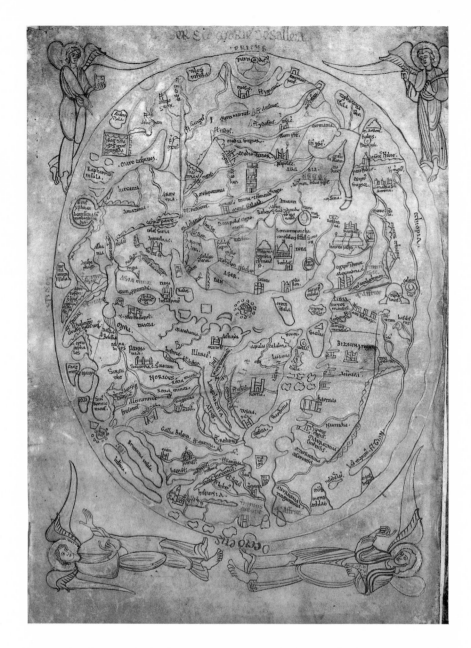

strangely elongated Black Sea — occur regularly. We find even its nearly circular Jutland on, for instance, some of the maps in the works of Isidore of Seville and Lambert of Saint-Omer. How far the Cotton map is a faithful copy of its Roman prototype we can only guess. The prototype may well have included the major European rivers, which appear on a number of medieval world maps but only in vestigial form on the Cotton map; and the Cotton map looks as if it may have suffered some distortion in being drawn to fit the particular page. On the other hand, what to our eyes seems one of its more distorted features, the way south-west Britain and north-west Spain are drawn close together, may well be faithful to the original, for some early medieval writers echo the belief that the British Isles were not far from Spain.

Where we might particularly look for the influence of the Cotton map —

or, rather, of its prototype — is in the group of world maps that mark the culmination of the early medieval tradition. Dating from the twelfth century to the fourteenth, they have long been recognised as a single interrelated group, though they do not all have the same antecedents and the relationships between them have not been fully worked out. They are very far from uniform. Even in size they differ enormously, ranging from the tiny Psalter map, less than 10 centimetres in diameter (20), to the huge Ebstorf map, greatest of all the medieval world maps, more than 3.5 metres across (21). In the larger ones the map was used, more than in any other medieval maps, as a vehicle for every kind of information, learned and moral, and the spatial element becomes little more than the framework of presentation. Many earlier world maps illustrated comprehensive encyclopaedias; these were practically encyclopaedias in themselves.

It is in this group of maps that the significance of the phrase *mappa mundi*, cloth of the world, becomes apparent, for although the survivors are all drawn on parchment we now see the world map being used as a freestanding work of art and learning, hung up on a wall or behind an altar as decoration, as a source of edification and instruction, or as a symbol of deity. One writer who used the phrase in the early thirteenth century was Gervase of Tilbury; it is significant that he was born in England, for all the maps in this group have English associations. That is not to say they were all produced in England. The Ebstorf map was unquestionably drawn in Germany. But it was arguably drawn at the behest of this same Gervase of Tilbury, now living in Germany; or of another Gervase whose origins are unknown but whose name was much more unusual in Germany than in contemporary England. The earliest map in the group was drawn in the early twelfth century, possibly by Henry, canon of Mainz Cathedral, for it illustrates his edition of an encyclopaedic chronicle of the world by Honorius of Autun; but he dedicated his work to another Henry, probably an Englishman, and the only surviving copy comes from the library of Sawley Abbey in Yorkshire (18).

All the other maps in the group are of English origin, including one that found its way to the cathedral library at Vercelli in north Italy, and it is clear that in the thirteenth century the large world map, the cloth of the world, was a peculiarly English genre. Besides those that survive we know of others, now lost, through references in contemporary writings: in the thirteenth century King Henry III had *mappae mundi* painted on the walls of his palaces at Westminster and Winchester, while Matthew Paris, monk at St Albans, mentions one that he saw at Waltham Abbey. More may still be discovered. During the last few years fragments of two of these English world maps, hitherto unknown, have come to light, both having been used in the sixteenth century as bindings for volumes of estate records, one by the college of Bonhommes at Ashridge in Hertfordshire, the other by Walter Aslake, owner of manors in north-west Norfolk (28). Enough of each survives to identify its date, its English origin and its relation to other maps in the group.

pages 26 and 27

19 Cotton world map

This small tenth- or eleventh-century English map, measuring 21 by 17 centimetres, probably offers the closest copy we have of a Roman map from which the outlines of many medieval world maps ultimately derive. The shape of north-west Europe, particularly the British Isles, is remarkable. Mountains are marked in green, and red is used not only for the Red Sea (top right) but also for the Persian Gulf, the Nile with its delta and other African rivers.
British Library, Cotton MS. Tiberius B.V, f.56v

20 Psalter world map

This map in a thirteenth-century English psalter compresses much information into a small area — it is less than 10 centimetres across — and is related to the large Ebstorf and Hereford maps. Like them it has Jerusalem at the centre and along the right-hand (southern) edge a series of pictures of monstrous races.
British Library, Additional MS. 28681, f.9

19

26

21 Ebstorf world map

The largest known medieval world map — it measured over 3 metres across — the Ebstorf map was destroyed in an air raid in 1943 but has been carefully reconstructed from earlier reproductions. Two portions of the map (top right and bottom left) had been lost before the map came to light in 1830 in the convent at Ebstorf, near Lüneburg, for which it had been drawn some 600 years earlier. At the edge of the map are the head, hands and feet of Christ.

Ebstorf, Kloster Ebstorf

22 Hereford world map

Though much smaller than the Ebstorf map, the Hereford map, 1.3 metres across, was likewise meant for display. The dark green of its seas and rivers stands out clearly. It was drawn by Richard of Holdingham, probably at Lincoln in the 1280s, being taken to Hereford soon after. Other large world maps in thirteenth-century England but now lost were at Westminster Palace, Winchester Castle and Waltham Abbey.

Hereford, Hereford Cathedral

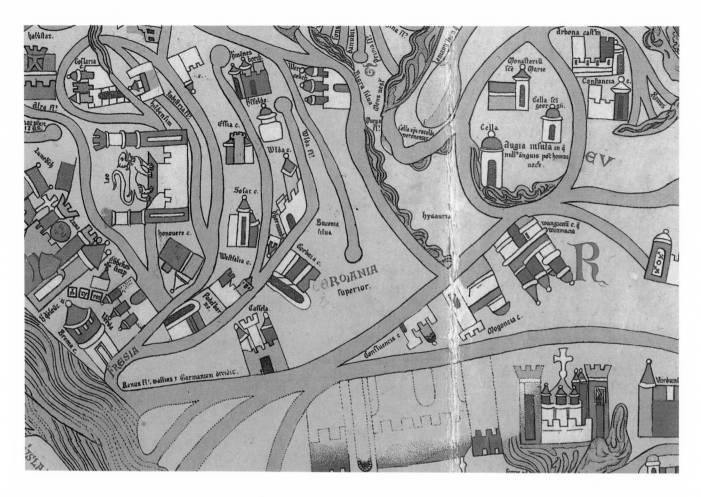

23 Germany on the Ebstorf world map

The Ebstorf map's details of German towns and rivers are unparalleled on any surviving medieval map. Centre left, with towers surmounted by a cross, a flag and the moon (*luna*) is Lüneburg, and just to its right is Ebstorf ('Ebbekes storp'). The three monastic buildings on the island at Reichenau (top right) probably also come from the compiler's own local knowledge.
Ebstorf, Kloster Ebstorf

24 North-west corner of the Hereford world map

In the bottom left corner, outside the map, the Roman Emperor Augustus orders three surveyors to measure the world. On the map itself is north-west Europe. Scotland is shown as an island and Ireland is divided in two by the River Boyne. In Germany rivers link the Danube with the North Sea.
Hereford, Hereford Cathedral

The giant Ebstorf map was destroyed in an air-raid on Hanover in 1943. Four full-size replicas have been made with scrupulous care, using surviving photographs as well as other evidence of the colouring of the original, so although physical examination of the map — its composition, its writing, its drawing — is no longer possible we have full access to its contents (21). The Hereford map (22) is now the largest surviving map of the group, but it is much smaller, only 1.3 metres across, so its area is thus only about one-seventh that of the Ebstorf map. They are not very closely related; the Hereford map is nearer to the map of Henry of Mainz, the Ebstorf map to the Vercelli and Psalter maps. Nor are they contemporary. The date as well as the authorship of the Ebstorf map is a matter of debate, but it belongs to the early or mid-thirteenth century and recently it has been convincingly argued that it dates from 1239; it was made at or for the convent at Ebstorf, near Lüneburg, and came to light there in 1832. The origin of the Hereford map is clearer, for it states unequivocally that it was produced by Richard of Holdingham, and doubts centre only on his exact identity and career; it was drawn probably at Lincoln in the 1280s, was taken to Hereford Cathedral soon after and, apart from short episodes, has been there ever since. In many obvious ways the maps differ. Thus Ebstorf (but not Hereford) has the head, hands and feet of Christ visible at top, sides and bottom of the map as though the world were his body, while Hereford (but not Ebstorf)

25 Africa on the Hereford world map

The river on the left is the Nile and towns marked on it include Alexandria, Memphis and Cairo ('Babilonia', on the lower of the two islands). But the information on large medieval world maps was not confined to geography, and we see here items taken from the Bible, romances and works of natural history, such as Joseph's barns and the mandrake (both left centre), the unicorn and the camp of Alexander the Great with its conical tents (both bottom centre). Comparison with **13**, part of the same area from the Ebstorf world map, shows how the two maps are alike in concept and general plan but very different in detail.
Hereford, Hereford Cathedral

has protruding labels bearing the letters M, O, R, S, death — a reminder of the limits of the material world. Again, to take examples of details, Ebstorf (but not Hereford) has a lifelike camel beside Jerusalem; Hereford (but not Ebstorf) has a charming mermaid in the eastern Mediterranean. But in concept and in the sources they use the two maps are very alike, and they bring together the non-geographical material that was drawn on, in a much more limited way, by the compilers of many lesser medieval world maps.

Foremost among these sources was of course the Bible. Both maps have Jerusalem at the centre — by no means all medieval world maps place it there — but on Ebstorf it is drawn with square walls enclosing a picture of the risen Christ while on Hereford it is circular with Christ crucified outside it. Among places or scenes from the Old Testament entered on both maps are the ark of Noah at Mount Ararat (with dove and olive branch on Ebstorf), Babylon with the tower of Babel beside it, and Mount Sinai beside the Red Sea (coloured red on Hereford, which shows Moses receiving the tablets of stone and marks the route taken by the people of Israel). From the New Testament both show the stable at Bethlehem, but only Ebstorf locates (just a few) incidents in the life of Christ. Both take material from the lives of the apostles and the early history of the church; thus Ebstorf shows the tomb of Bartholomew with a lamp burning above while Hereford shows Augustine standing in the church at Hippo. Much, as we would expect, was drawn from writings about distant lands — descriptive, moral, historical and literary (**13**, **25**). Among them were Pliny's *Natural History*, which describes mythical races of monstrous beings, such as the dog-headed cynocephali or the sciopods who used their one enormous foot as a shade from the sun; the *Physiologus*, a third- or fourth-century compilation which sets out the moral lessons to be learned from the ways of such strange creatures as the phoenix or the pelican; and the medieval romance of Alexander the Great, with its account, embellished with marvels, of his travels to India.

Some of the most interesting details on these maps were drawn from the contemporary world of the compilers. Many towns in Europe are marked and named. It has been shown that places in France on the Hereford map come from a series of medieval itineraries — a route used by Florentine merchants to carry English wool from Bordeaux to north Italy, the pilgrim route to Compostella and other routes from north to south (**24**). The Ebstorf map, unlike Hereford, shows a great many towns in Germany, perhaps taken from a series of river-based itineraries (**23**). It also has some local detail that seems to come from the compiler's personal knowledge: at Reichenau, near Constance, where the abbey and two monastic cells appear, and at Ebstorf itself, where we see not only the convent with spire and cross, but also its five martyrs' graves, the subject of a developing cult in the thirteenth century. On the other hand the Ebstorf map makes a nonsense of Germany's river system by linking the Weser and the Main; like even worse mistakes on the Hereford map, which seems to join both Weser and Elbe to the Danube, this probably arose from mistaking mountains for rivers when the

34

26 World map by Ranulf Higden

Higden, a monk at Chester in the fourteenth century, compiled a
popular universal history. Some of the 120 surviving manuscript
copies are illustrated by a world map, but its form and shape
vary — on some it is circular, on some a pointed oval, on some a
rounded oval, as on this late-fourteenth-century example, where
it occupies a double page, 46 by 34 centimetres. The heads
around the map represent the twelve winds. In Britain (lower
left) there are more town symbols than in all the rest of Europe.
British Library, Royal MS. 14 C.IX, ff.1v-2

27 World map by Pietro Vesconte

Vesconte, working in Venice, brought into his world maps the
relatively accurate outline of the Mediterranean and Black Sea
that had developed on portolan charts. On this map, 35
centimetres across, compiled about 1320, this area is thus more
easily recognised than on earlier world maps. From portolan
charts Vesconte also took the rhumb lines that cover the whole
of the map's surface.
British Library, Additional MS. 27376*, ff.187v-188

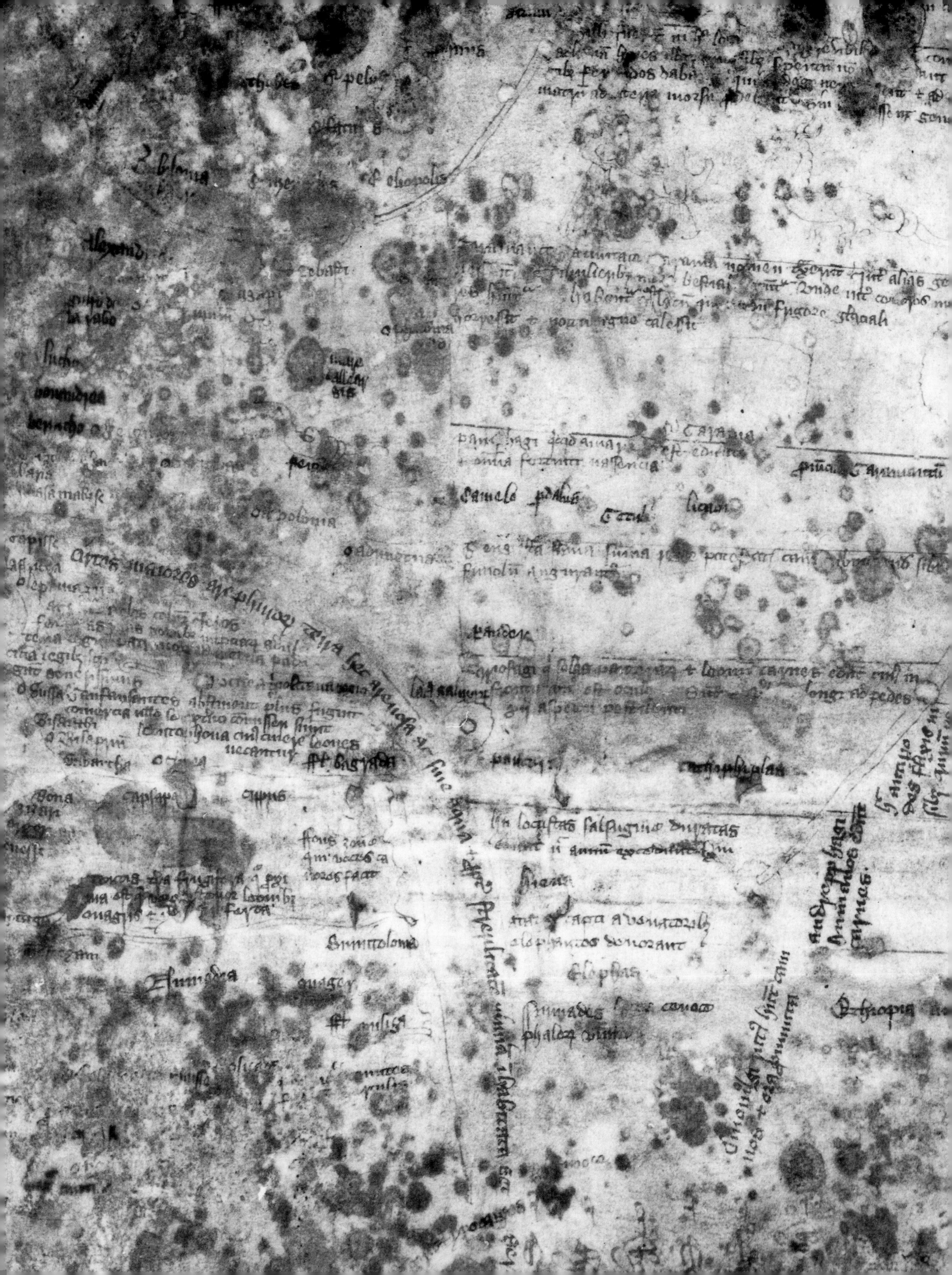

Ethiopes p̄ peles

Babilonia ḡ mgʳ... p̄ Eliopolis

Alexandʳ

...de la valle

... Suches
communidꝰ
bennacho...
...lapa
...sa malise

...pisse

Aↄtes maiores ẏ plunq̄ ...ṁ p̄cuiꝰ ...iꝑa sic ꝗcūq̄ ar sue ...na
eloplices ...

Camele pᵉ... cenᵘ ligno

pander

Ista locusta salugno ...ptas
...rū ...ū ...

Esmirolonia
quater
pᵗ ...lis

Esmirides
phalꝫ ...

Ethiopia

28 Part of Africa on the Aslake
world map
This recently discovered fragment of a
fourteenth-century English world map
was used as a cover for late-medieval
records of a Norfolk estate and may have
come from Creake Abbey. Though badly
damaged — the photograph was taken
under ultra-violet light — it is of great
interest, not least in the African
place-names that it drew from some
unidentified portolan chart. On this
portion names just visible beyond the
curving line of the Nile (top left) include
'Babilonia' (i.e. Cairo) and 'Eoliopolis'
(Heliopolis).
British Library, Additional MS. 63841A

map was set out. The compiler's own observation of the part of the world
he knew really played a negligible part in the construction of either map.

More or less elaborate diagram-maps in the tradition of the early medieval world maps were still being produced in the fourteenth and fifteenth
centuries. One of them — in various versions — appears in copies of a
compendious and immensely popular history book, the Polychronicon,
written in the mid-fourteenth century by Ranulf Higden, monk at Chester
(**26**). That he was English may be significant given the English associations
of the group of world maps that includes the Ebstorf and Hereford maps.

Yet if we look at the world maps that Pietro Vesconte was drawing at
Venice in the 1320s the scene suddenly changes. The Mediterranean and the
Black Sea are no longer an unrecognisable pattern of shapes that can be
identified only by the names attached to them; instead we see, more or less
accurately drawn, the outline that we are familiar with today (**27**). This
reflects the advent of the portolan chart, and indeed even the Aslake map,
firmly linked as it is with the Ebstorf, Hereford and, especially, the Psalter
maps, takes the Canary Islands and the places it names along the African
coast from a portolan chart of about 1350 (**28**). The development of the
portolan chart was crucial to the development of the world map in the later
middle ages.

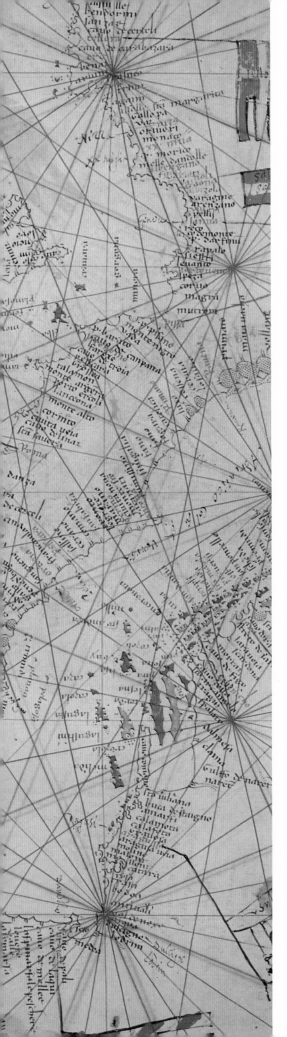

CHAPTER THREE

Portolan charts before 1400

I
N the summer of 1270 Louis IX, king of France, sailed across the Mediterranean on crusade to Tunis. On the way the ships of his fleet were scattered in a storm and the king asked his ship's officers how far they were from Cagliari in Sardinia. The chronicler Guillaume de Nangis, writing in Latin, tells how they thereupon brought a *mappa mundi* on which they showed him Cagliari and the area of the coast near to where they lay. This *mappa mundi* can hardly have been one of the contemporary world maps; in fact it is the earliest known reference to a portolan chart. The earliest surviving portolan chart dates from some twenty or thirty years later; it is known as the *carte pisane* because it was thought to have come from a family archive at Pisa (30). Some thirty portolan charts survive from the fourteenth century and about 150 from the fifteenth.

The basis of every portolan chart is a simple coastal outline of the Mediterranean and the Black Sea, though it might be extended to include the west European coast as far as the British Isles and the North Sea, ultimately even to the Baltic and the west coast of Africa. Essentially it was a sea chart, used in navigation. Few, if any, inland features are shown, the many coastal place-names are written on the land side of the coastline so as not to obscure possible danger points, and prominent headlands may be slightly exaggerated. A distinctive feature is the network of so-called rhumb lines that cover the map. At first sight they seem almost arbitrarily drawn but in fact they conform to a careful pattern. Sixteen equidistant points,

29 Italy on a portolan chart by Pietro Vesconte
The detail and general accuracy of their coastal outline set portolan charts apart from all other medieval maps before the fifteenth century. This example by Pietro Vesconte, who worked in Venice, was copied about 1330. As on many portolan charts from Italy no inland features at all are shown, but flags mark some of the principal powers along the coast.
British Library, Additional MS. 27376*, f.181v

pages 40 and 41
30 *Carte pisane*
Portolan charts, maps of the Mediterranean used in navigation, originated in the mid-thirteenth century. The *carte pisane*, a damaged sheet of parchment some 50 by 100 centimetres, dates from the end of the century and is the oldest known to survive. Besides the portolan chart's usual rhumb lines, joining points on one or (as here) two large circles, the *carte pisane* has several areas covered by small rectangular grids of unknown purpose.
Paris, Bibliothèque Nationale, Rés.Ge. B1118

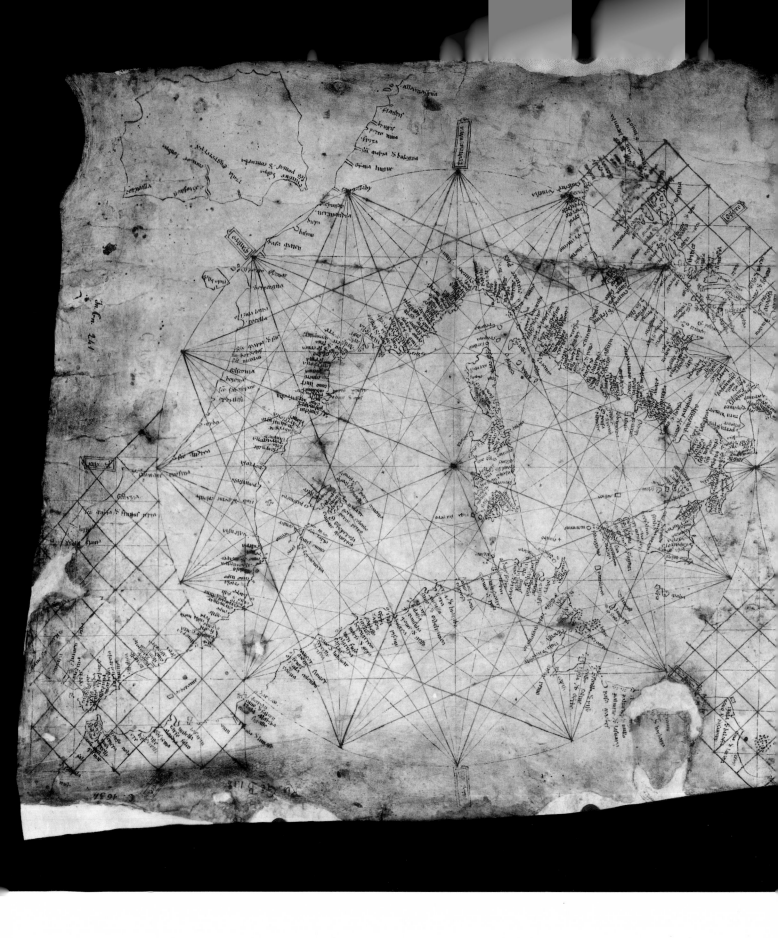

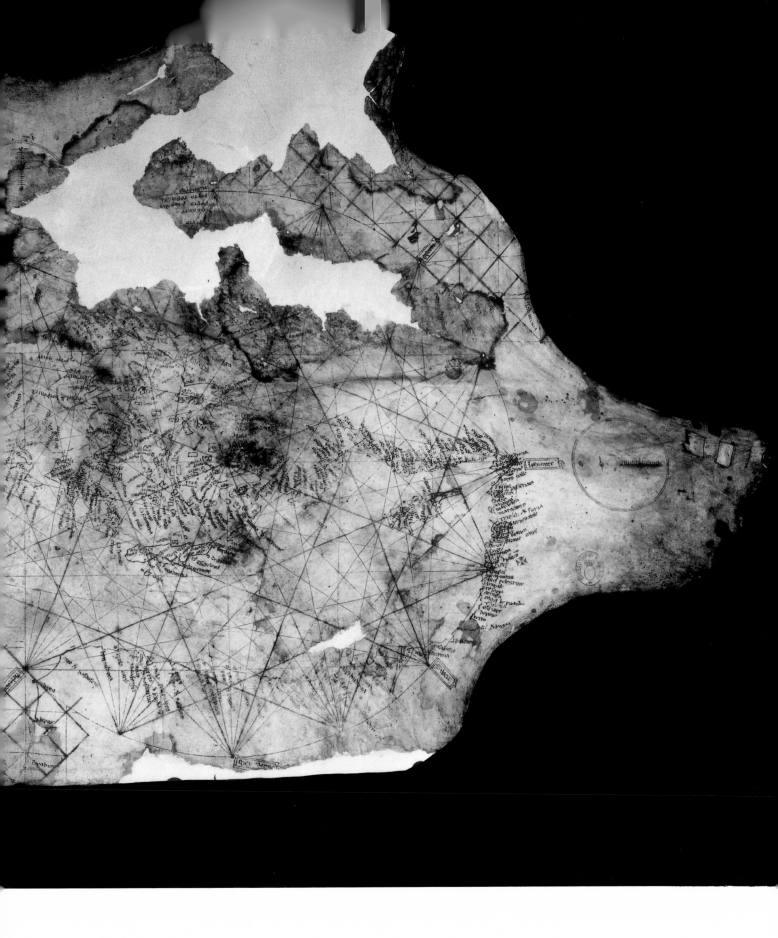

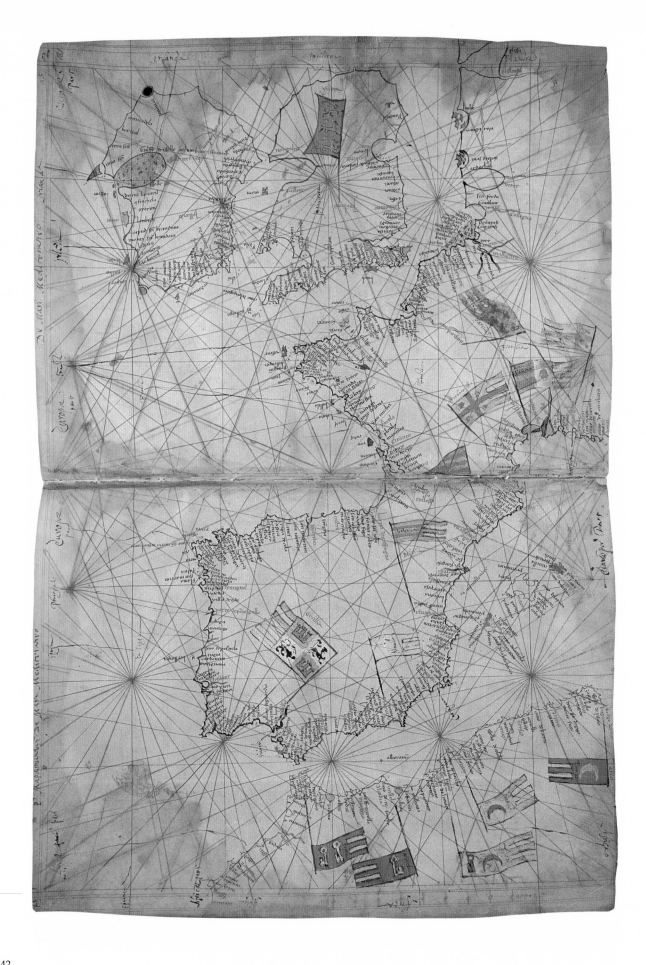

31 Portolan chart of western Europe by Pietro Vesconte

Portolan charts were primarily of the Mediterranean and Black Sea, but were soon extended to include Europe's Atlantic coast. It is interesting to compare Vesconte's chart with the *carte pisane*, some twenty years older (**30**), which has here no more than an inaccurately sketched outline. The coastal outlines of portolan charts developed in a continuous process of adjustment and improvement. Here it is notable how the coasts regularly followed by Mediterranean ships — Portugal, the Bay of Biscay, the English Channel — are far more accurately drawn than those they seldom visited.
British Library, Additional MS. 27376*, ff.180v-181

32 Map in the margin of Dati, *The Sphere*

Manuscripts of *The Sphere*, a poem in Italian by Gregorio Dati (1362-1435) or his brother Leonardo, are decorated with maps based on portolan charts. On these pages from a copy written about 1470 the map has east at the top. At the foot of the right-hand page are the east end of the Mediterranean and Cairo ('Karo') on the River Nile. Above them are Syria and Mesopotamia, with the Persian Gulf, Arabia and the Red Sea — coloured red — on the right.
British Library, Additional MS. 22329, ff. 17v-18

among them the four cardinal points, would be marked along the circumference of a large notional circle; actual lines then joined (and extended beyond) all these points. Sometimes the basic circle is actually drawn on the map and sometimes there are two circles, not one — both are the case on the *carte pisane*.

The word *portolano* is Italian and means written sailing directions. The earliest medieval compilation of this sort that we have for the Mediterranean dates from the mid-thirteenth century. But despite the coincidence of dates there is nothing to suggest that portolan charts were directly

33 Morocco on a portolan chart by Petrus Rosselli

Rosselli was perhaps Italian in origin, but it was in Majorca that he produced his
portolan charts in the mid-fifteenth century — this example dates from 1465. It
follows, more elaborately than Dulcert's chart a century earlier (**34**), the Catalan
tradition of introducing inland features to the chart. Here, within the workmanlike
outline of Morocco's Atlantic coast (top left) are not only the main inland cities — Fez
('Fes'), Marrakesh ('Morochs') — but further towns and rivers south of the Atlas
Mountains.

British Library, Egerton MS. 2712

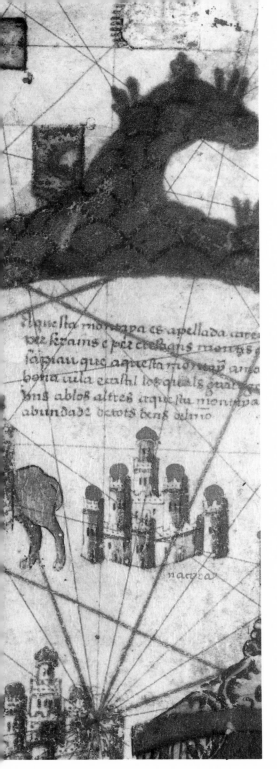

connected with this or any other *portolano*; the term portolan chart is a modern invention and unnecessary confusion has been caused by sometimes calling them simply portolans. Certainly the portolan charts we know from the fourteenth and fifteenth centuries are independent of the written *portolani* — most are unattached to any text. Some are drawn on single sheets of parchment, others form small books or atlases, each page covering a different area.

It is clear from contemporary writers — Guillaume de Nangis among them — that portolan charts were taken to sea and were regarded as practical aids to navigation, perhaps with the help of dividers. But just how they were used is far from clear. Surviving charts betray no obvious traces of use in this way and they may have served mostly as a simple aide-mémoire, a handy guide to the features of coasts that were seldom out of sight for long on Mediterranean voyages. On the other hand some portolan charts were what we might call library copies, perhaps drawn with this in mind and never meant to be taken to sea. These must be disproportionately represented among portolan charts surviving today. Apart from suffering less wear and tear than one would expect on board ship they will have been more ornate and thus more likely to be kept.

No less mysterious than how it was used is how the portolan chart originated. Much research and learned debate has done little to solve this problem and the fullest recent discussion reaches no firm conclusion. We can be fairly sure that portolan charts really did first appear in the mid-thirteenth century: since surviving charts and references to others suddenly start to appear then, it is unlikely that we are dealing with the first survivors of a much older tradition. But we cannot rule out the possibility that the portolan charts all stem from a map of classical origin; it may have suddenly come to light or some imaginative person may have grasped the possibilities it presented. It is just possible — but not at all likely — that this map was based on those in Claudius Ptolemy's *Geography*, otherwise unknown in western Europe until the fifteenth century; certainly it was unrelated to whatever classical prototype lay behind the Cotton world map, which presents a quite different view of the Mediterranean. Probably, though, the first portolan chart was an entirely new compilation, produced not from astronomical observations and geographical coordinates but simply from carefully measuring, recording and collating the direction and distance of a great many voyages. It is significant that the magnetic compass first appeared in the Mediterranean in the twelfth century and came into general use there in the thirteenth.

Whether they derived from a new map or from a classical model, the earliest portolan charts were rapidly improved through observation and experience. We see this happening quite dramatically in the way the British Isles are shown on fourteenth-century charts. By the 1320s the simple rectangle that represented Britain on the *carte pisane* had developed into a more recognisable shape and Ireland had been added beside it. But this was an outlying area, likely to be corrected at a late stage; the finer adjustments

34 Portolan chart attributed to Angelino Dulcert

This mid-fourteenth-century portolan chart is unsigned but may be by Angelino Dulcert. Certainly it is in the style associated with Catalan charts. Unlike Italian ones a few inland features are shown — prominent here, for instance, are the Atlas Mountains and the Alps, a few rivers including the Danube and the Guadalquivir, and a church marking Rome.

British Library, Additional MS. 25691

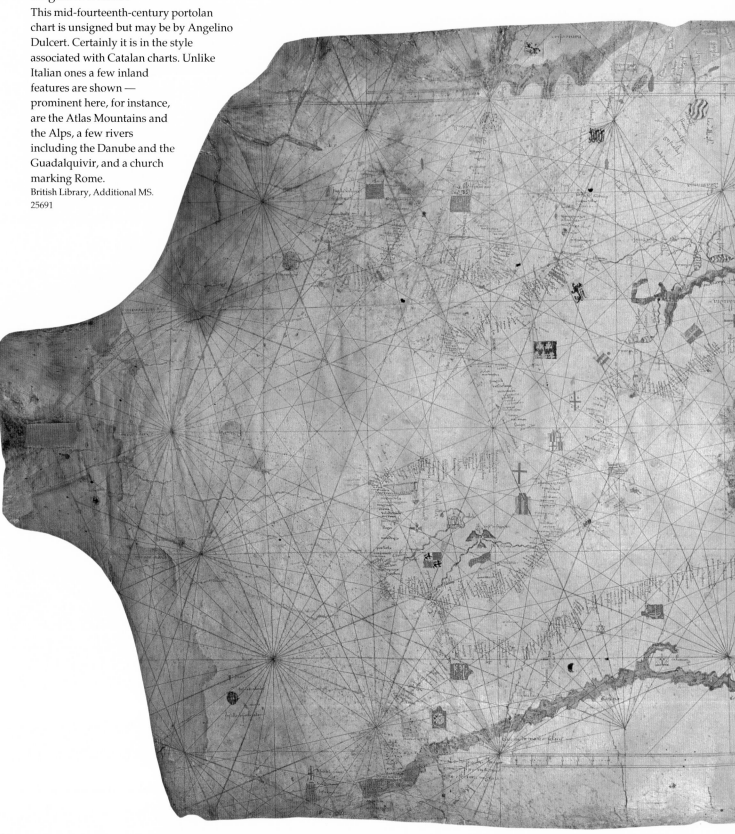

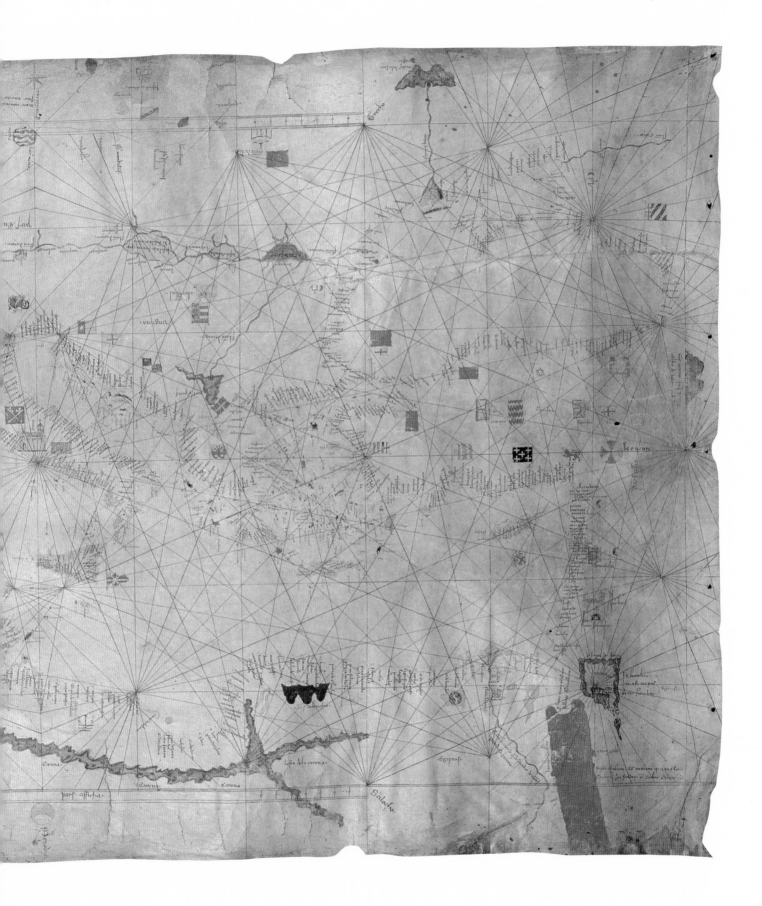

Veneto, *Great Chronology*
This manuscript was produced about 1320
at Naples, but the map of Italy may well
owe its inspiration to Pietro Vesconte of
Venice. Drawn with south at the top and
arbitrarily divided into north and south
portions, it occupies two facing pages of
the book. The coasts are taken from
portolan charts, but inland features —
mountains, rivers, towns — have been
added. The lack of names in west central
Italy suggests that the map is unfinished.
Rome, Biblioteca Apostolica Vaticana, MS. Vat.lat.
1960, f.267v

that we see being made in the Mediterranean outline over the same period
may be no more than the last stage in a process that, starting from a crude
beginning, had produced a tolerably good map by the time the *carte pisane*
first reveals it to us. By then, we should remember, portolan charts had been
known for at least twenty years, quite possibly for thirty or fifty.

The early appearance of scale-bars and direction indicators on the portolan charts shows how important the accurate measurement of distance
and direction was to those who drew them and to those who used them.
The first scale-bars, on early-fourteenth-century charts, are placed within a
circle; but before long a simple bar, often at the margin, became normal. It
might be thought that no direction indicator was needed beyond the rhumb
lines, which always included north-south and east-west alignments, but a
miniature compass rose appears on a portolan atlas of 1375 and frequently
in portolan charts of the fifteenth century; the markings on the compass
itself may well have derived from the nodal points of the rhumb lines on a
chart.

These were not the only changes made on portolan charts in the course
of the fourteenth century. The number of places named along the coasts

steadily increases on the earliest charts, but after about 1325 most have some 1100 or 1200 names of which more than a third might vary from one chart to another. These changes may reflect the changing pattern of Mediterranean settlement and commerce, as one little coastal town grew in importance and another declined, but their detailed significance has not been worked out. They can only be an uncertain guide to the chronology of change, for where a particular development can be dated it seldom appears rapidly on a chart and sometimes only after a very long interval. Bilbao, founded about 1300, appears on a chart by 1339; Villefranche, built in 1295, does not replace the site's old name, Olivule, on the charts until the mid-fifteenth century. The same applies to the flags that appear along the coasts on many of the charts to show who held local lordship. A chart of about 1385 is the first to show the English flag with the fleurs-de-lis that were added to it in 1340, and Montpellier, acquired by France from Aragon in 1349, first appears with the French emblems on its flag in 1426.

Long debate over where the earliest portolan charts were made has produced more heat than light, but those surviving from the first half of the fourteenth century certainly include charts made at Palma, Genoa and Venice. At this date, where it was made scarcely affected the contents of a chart — all gave more or less the same information and any changes were copied on maps made anywhere. After about 1350, however, the different places of origin developed their own traditions, and it starts to become possible to say where a map was drawn from the particular place-names and other features that it shows. In general style, however, Italian maps can be distinguished earlier than this from Spanish ones. Broadly speaking (there are exceptions) Italian maps showed nothing beyond what was relevant to navigation — coastlines and coastal settlements — while the Catalan ones showed some inland features — rivers and mountains — and were more likely to include vignettes and other decoration.

Most of the early portolan charts are anonymous, but some of the mapmakers can be identified and one deserves special mention — Pietro Vesconte, who came from Genoa but did some, perhaps all, of his work at Venice (29, 31). His work falls within the period 1310-30; the name Perrino Vesconte, which appears on one atlas and one chart, may be his own, using a diminutive form, or that of another member of his family. Vesconte was one of the few people in Europe before 1400 to see the potential of cartography and to apply its techniques with imagination. We have already seen that in the world maps he drew around 1320 he introduced the outline of the Mediterranean and Black Sea taken from the portolan charts. We may suspect that his influence lay behind the maps of Italy in the *Great Chronology* by Paolino Veneto that was copied at Naples not long after (35), for other maps in the same manuscript are related to maps from Vesconte's workshop that illustrate Marino Sanudo's book calling for a new crusade. These maps of Italy use the coastal outline from portolan charts as the basis for a general map of the area, showing mountains, rivers and inland towns. It was a precursor of the use of portolan charts in regional mapping.

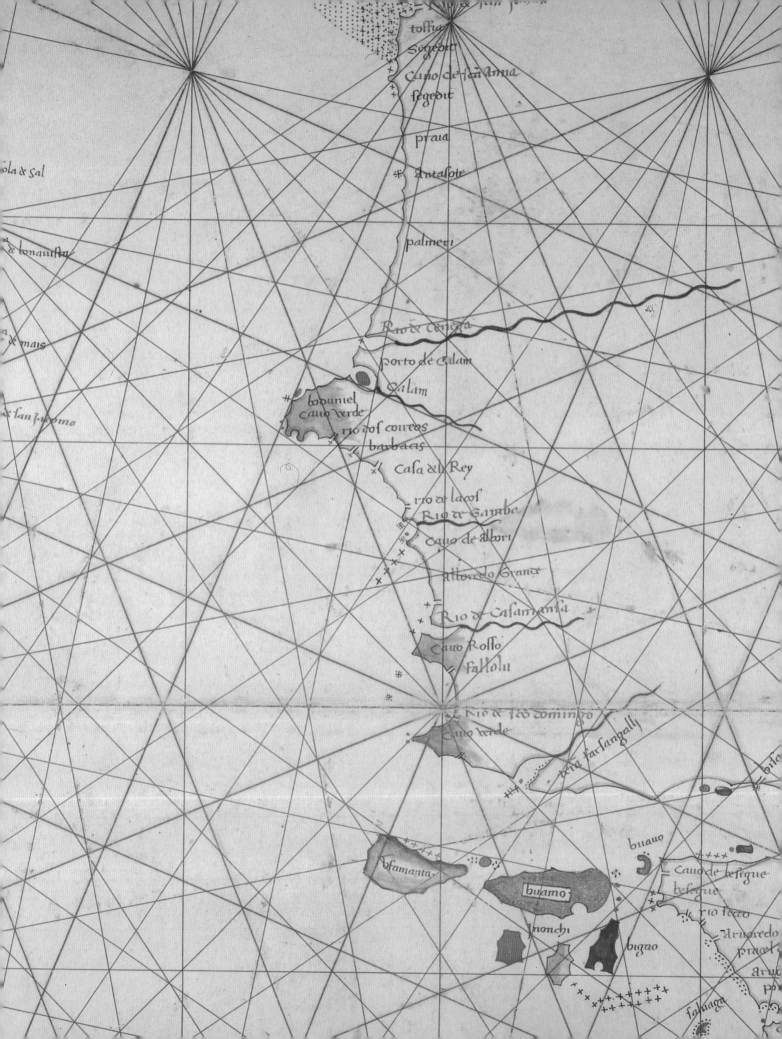

The fifteenth century

THREE developments in the fifteenth century particularly affected the content of world maps and portolan charts. The first was the translation into Latin of Ptolemy's *Geography*. The second was the growth of philosophical interest in theoretical geography, in the calculation of geographical coordinates and their use in constructing maps. The third was the succession of voyages along the African coast, culminating in Bartolomeo Dias rounding the Cape of Good Hope in 1488 and presaging voyages of exploration still further afield, in the new world as well as the old. We have seen that already in the early fourteeenth century Pietro Vesconte used portolan charts in constructing a world map; in the fifteenth century this kind of cross-fertilisation between the two sorts of map became much more common, but it was still an occasional rather than a regular occurrence. At the end of the century these two traditions of map-making were still distinct; a single general pool of geographical information and cartographic expertise was just starting to come into being, to be drawn on alike by the portolan chart makers and the compilers of world maps.

Claudius Ptolemy worked in Alexandria in the early and mid-second century AD and we know of him only through his writings on a variety of scientific subjects. Among these is the work known from the Arabic version of its title as the *Almagest*, which catalogues over a thousand stars, defining the position of each and explaining how to construct a celestial globe. His *Geography* can be seen as a logical sequel. It gives the latitude and longitude of places, ideally from astronomical observation, as a basis for drawing maps of individual regions and of the whole world, and discusses possible ways of projecting the curved surface of the world on to the flat surface of a map. Ptolemy saw the world as a complete sphere, but the inhabited area as only a part of it, stretching south some 16 degrees beyond the Equator, north to about the Arctic Circle, east a little beyond Malaya, and bounded on the west by the Atlantic. Although his lists locate places by their geographical coordinates it is clear that these did not all come from immediate observation but were worked out from whatever information was available, such as accounts of journeys giving distances from one place to another; this means that their appearance of great accuracy is often spurious.

The oldest surviving manuscript of Ptolemy's Greek text was copied more than a thousand years after he wrote; it dates from the late twelfth or early thirteenth century. Enough other copies survive from the thirteenth and fourteenth centuries to show that it was — perhaps had suddenly become — a popular work in the Byzantine Greek cultural world (38). Some, not all, of these manuscripts include maps, and of these there are two versions. In both there is a world map, but one has 64 regional maps while the other, following Ptolemy's text more literally, has 26. These maps may or may not have been compiled by Ptolemy himself. His book gives instructions for making the maps but does not say in so many words that he has actually drawn them. They may have been constructed from the text and added to the book by a copyist at any date between Ptolemy's own time and

36 Part of chart of the west African coast by Grazioso Benincasa

An important innovation on fifteenth-century maps was the record of new discoveries made on voyages beyond Europe. This detail, from an atlas of charts that Grazioso Benincasa produced at Venice in 1473, shows Cape Verde (the upper of the two green capes named 'Cauo Verde'), the Gambia River ('Rio de Gamba'), Cape Roxo ('Cauo Rosso', coloured red) and the Bissagos Archipelago.

British Library, Egerton MS. 2855, ff.6v-7

the earliest known manuscripts. There is also some reason to suppose that the world map was constructed separately from the regional maps of either version.

It was a text with maps that was translated into Latin by Jacobus Angelus in about 1406 and first introduced Ptolemy's *Geography* into western Europe. Its impact is shown by the number of surviving fifteenth-century manuscripts of the Latin version (41, 42) and by the succession of early printed editions. The first, at Vicenza in 1475, had no maps, but it was then published with maps at Bologna in 1477, Rome in 1478 (40) and 1490, Ulm in 1482 and 1486, and so on. It is shown too by the way other world maps quickly assimilated elements from Ptolemy's. Thus the map copied by Pirrus de Noha about 1414 to illustrate a quite different geographical text of the Roman period, the *Chorography* of the first-century author Pomponius Mela, takes from Ptolemy its land-locked Indian Ocean, the shapes of Malaya and Sri Lanka (*Taprobana*) and much else. Much later in the century we see Ptolemy's influence just as clearly in the world maps of Henricus Martellus, who was working at Florence in the 1480s and 1490s (39). But not all world maps were affected. We see little trace of the Ptolemy maps in Andrea Bianco's world map of 1436 or in the Vinland map which — whether drawn in the fifteenth century or the twentieth — is closely related; instead we see the portolan charts and the tradition represented by the Cotton map.

In fact, although this will not have been apparent in the fifteenth century, the Ptolemy maps, while impressive in their detail and their scope, were not so very much better than those already available in western Europe. With hindsight and a knowledge of correct coastal outlines, we can see this in the Ptolemy map of Britain. It is closer to reality than the Cotton map in the shape it gives east, south-east and north-west England, but in south-west England and Scotland the Cotton map is more accurate. Indeed, the outline of Scotland on the Ptolemy map is spectacularly wrong, with an eastern protuberance extending far towards Denmark; this feature appears on many later maps down to the sixteenth century so that, for instance, Scotland protrudes on to the maps of Germany with north Italy that Erhard Etzlaub published at Nuremberg probably in 1500 and in 1501. Again, the portolan charts of the early fifteenth century had achieved a better coastal outline of Italy than the Ptolemy map.

The importance of the Ptolemy maps does not lie in their accuracy, which people in the fifteenth century could not easily assess. Partly it lay in the detailed coverage of maps and text alike — they were systematic and comprehensive. But much more it lay in the merits of the method, irrespective of the accuracy of the information. Any of the geographical coordinates could be checked, however crudely, by actual observation and corrected. Ptolemy's text could be seen as a starting point for a process of correction and improvement. Moreover, by defining so many fixed points it provided a check on the accurate copying of the maps. Ptolemy's maps may — or may not — have been copied for a thousand years before the earliest known manuscript; but insofar as the locations of the places they name accord with

38 Claudius Ptolemy's world map in Greek

Ptolemy's *Geography* was well known in the Greek-speaking world long before the first Latin translation in the early fifteenth century. Even so, the oldest surviving copy was made more than a thousand years after Ptolemy wrote in the second century AD and it may be that Ptolemy's maps were first drawn in the middle ages from his listed geographical coordinates. This copy of the world map is in a fifteenth-century manuscript of the Greek text.

British Library, Additional MS. 19391, ff.17v-18

the lists of coordinates we know that they differ little from their prototypes. This is very different from, say, the Cotton map, where we have no fixed points, only a shape that might all too easily be distorted either by careless copying or by ill-judged attempts to edit and amend the outline; we need not doubt that the Cotton map had an ancient prototype, but we can do little more than guess how far it reproduces that prototype's actual appearance.

We see how the newly discovered Ptolemy stimulated new geographical work in a manuscript of the *Geography* that was prepared in 1427 for Cardinal Guillaume Fillastre, the aged French humanist scholar and expert in canon law. An extra regional map has been added, of Scandinavia (**43**), an area represented in Ptolemy's work only by Denmark. A corresponding section has been added to the text, listing some 130 places in Scandinavia with their coordinates, and both list and map are ascribed to the work of Claudius Clavus. A slightly later version of the written text is also known, but without a map; however, the influence of the Scandinavian map based on this revised list of coordinates has been traced in later world maps. Clavus was Danish, but he was living in Rome and his information was far from reliable. Nonetheless his map and lists are of great interest, partly as a first attempt to improve and expand the work of Ptolemy, partly because they extended mapping into an area beyond the limits of the portolan charts, an area to which world maps did less than justice.

Scientifically more respectable than Clavus's work, but probably even less influential, was the work on geographical coordinates that a small group of scholars carried out in the 1420s and 1430s at Vienna and nearby Klosterneuburg. It was part of a much larger sequence of astronomical and mathematical work, and it took as its starting point not the work of Ptolemy but the so-called Toledo tables, compiled in Arab Spain in the eleventh century. Of its products there survive only a couple of diagrams plotting the positions of places on a grid of latitude and longitude, coordinate tables for constructing world maps, and fragments of a few rough sketch maps. The importance of the work lies not so much in what was achieved as in its recognition of the method's theoretical value; but theoretical value was mostly all it could have in an age when, for want of mechanical time-pieces, simple measurement on the ground — dead reckoning — was the only practicable way of measuring longitude.

However, the ideas embodied in the Ptolemy maps were carried forward by a small number of maps, drawn with latitude and longitude, to

39 World map by Henry Martellus
The world maps of Henry Martellus, who worked at Florence, exemplify many of the fifteenth-century's developments in map-making. In this example the Mediterranean, western Europe and the west coast of Africa all derive from portolan charts, extended to take in the recent discovery of the Cape of Good Hope, rounded by Bartolomeo Dias in 1488. The rest of the map comes from Ptolemy, with some additions such as the outline of Scandinavia.
British Library, Additional MS. 15760, ff.68v-69

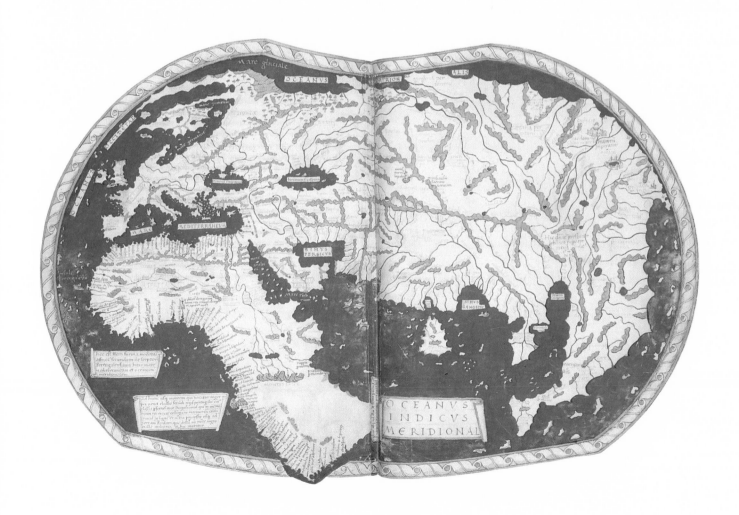

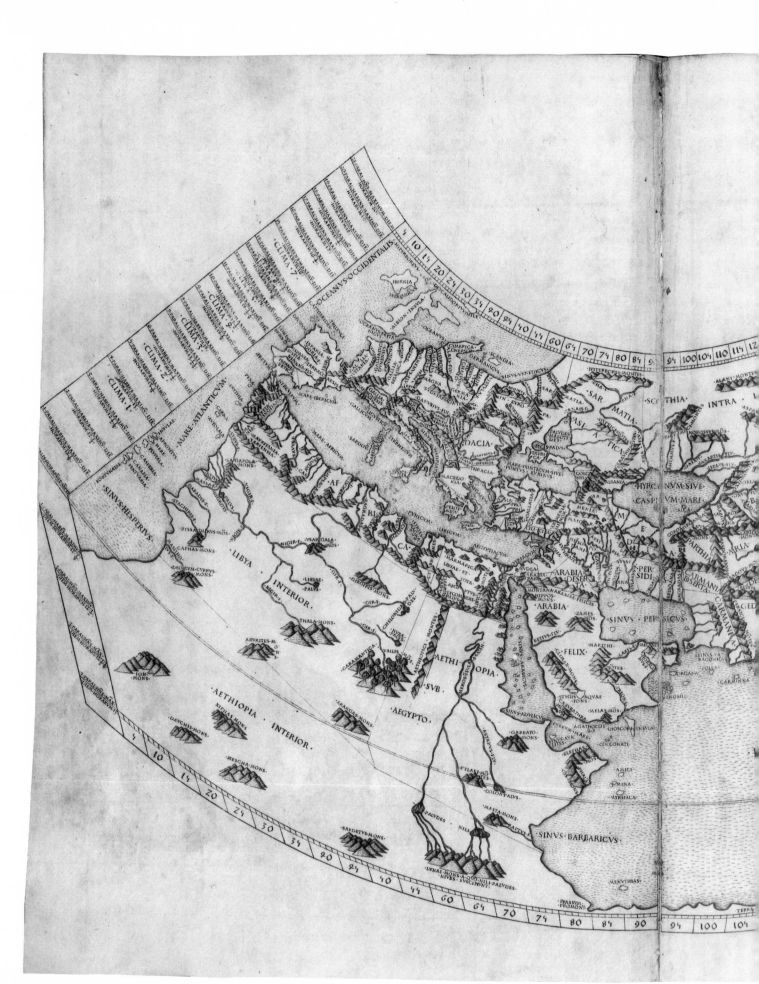

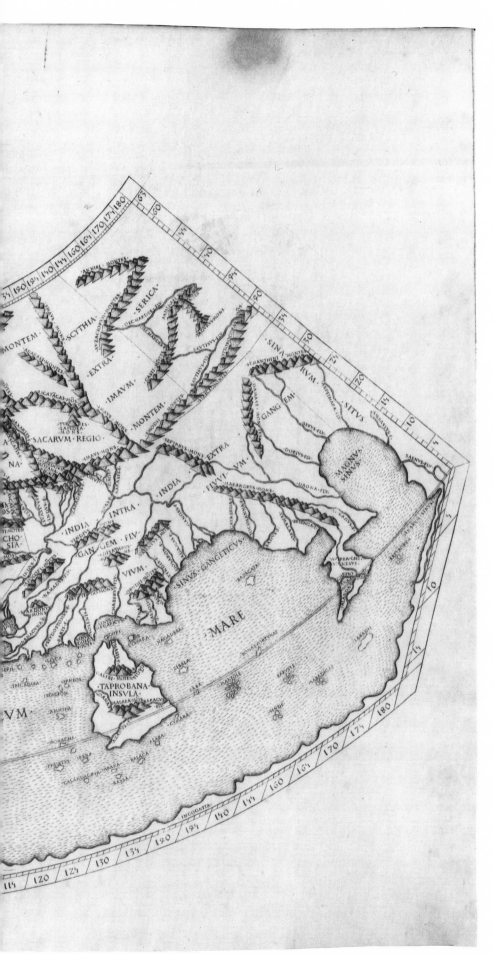

**40 Claudius Ptolemy's world map
in Latin, printed**

The *Geography* of Ptolemy, with its world
map and maps of individual regions,
became immensely popular in western
Europe once it had been translated from
Greek into Latin at the beginning of the
fifteenth century. Many manuscript copies
survive and it was first printed (at first
without maps) in 1475. This is the world
map from the edition published at Rome
in 1478. The strange shape of Scotland
(top left) is one of the odder features of the
Ptolemy maps.
British Library, C.3.d.6, map 1

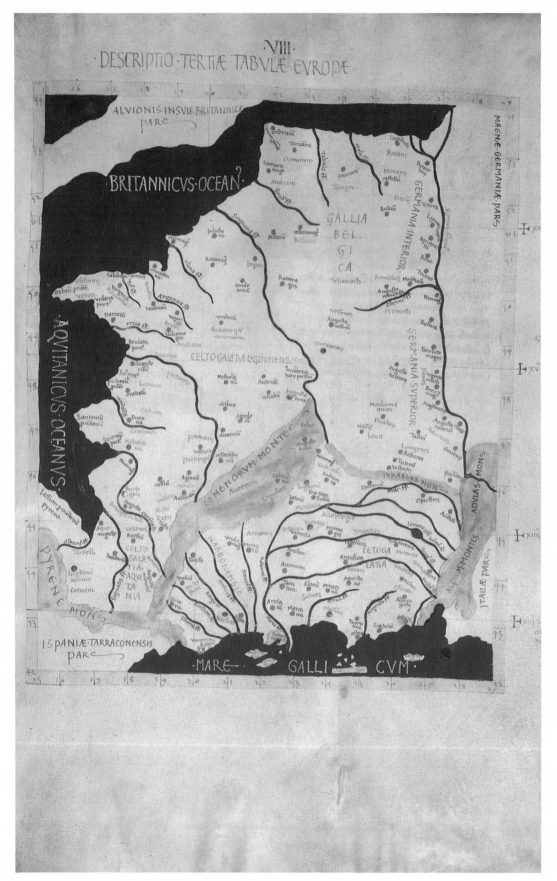

·VIII·
DESCRIPTIO·TERTIÆ·TABVLÆ·EVROPÆ·

ALVIONIS·INSVLÆ·BRITANNICÆ PARC

BRITANNICVS·OCEAN?

MAGNÆ·GERMANIÆ·PARS

GALLIA BEL GI CA

GERMANIA·INTERIOR

AQVITANICVS·OCEANVS·

CELTOGALATIA·LVGDVNENSIS

GERMANIA·SVPERIOR

CEMENORVM·MONTES

IVRASSVS·MONS

ADVIAS·MONS

NARBONENSIS

CETOGA LATIA

ALPINI·MONTES

ITALIÆ·PARS

PYRENE MONS

CELTO GALA TIA AQVI TA NIA

ISPANIÆ·TARRACONENSIS PARC

MARE GALLI CVM

41 Claudius Ptolemy's map of France

This map of France, measuring some 38 by 33 centimetres, is one of the 26 regional maps in a fifteenth-century manuscript of the Latin version of Ptolemy's *Geography*. It exemplifies the strength and the weakness of Ptolemy's maps. Positions of places are determined by geographical coordinates, and degrees of latitude and longitude are entered in the margin. But the coordinates were often incorrect, and contemporary portolan charts offered a more accurate map of the French Atlantic coast.
British Library, Harley MS. 7182, f.64

42 Claudius Ptolemy's map of the Bay of Bengal

This map is from a manuscript of Ptolemy's *Geography* very similar in date and size to that from which the map of France is taken. In this copy, however, the sea is consistently coloured yellow instead of blue. At the centre of the map is the Ganges delta, the Malay Peninsula is bottom right and among the places between them are Bassein and the Bassein River in Burma ('besinga', 'besingas fl''). At the foot are islands of cannibals ('anthropophagorum').
British Library, Harley MS. 7195, f.102v

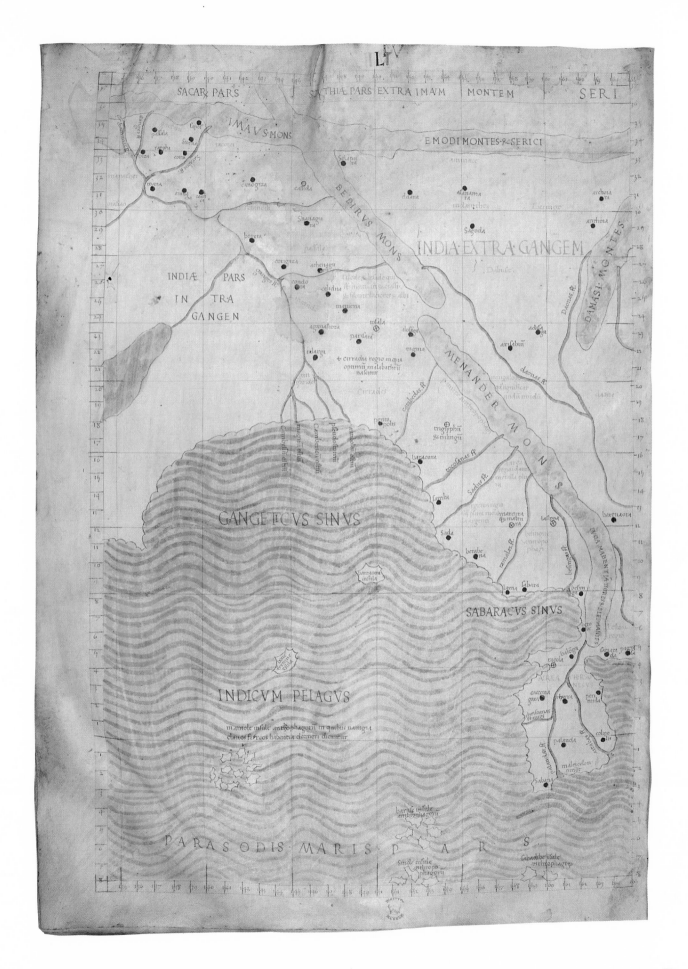

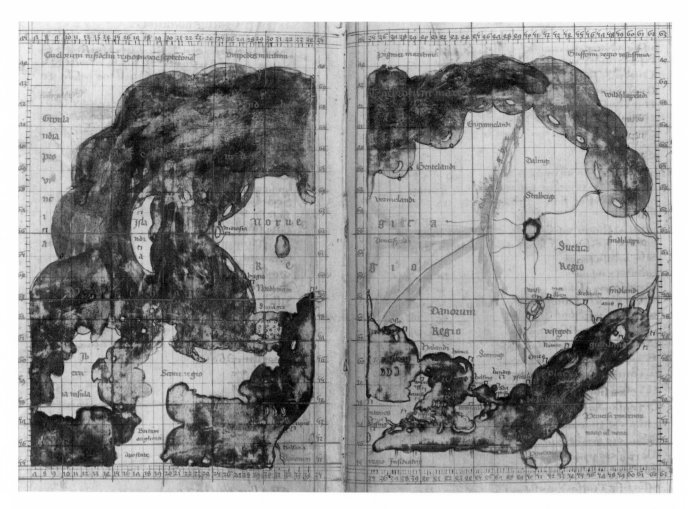

43 Map of Scandinavia by Claudius Clavus

Claudius Clavus, a Dane living in Rome, drew this map of Scandinavia to supplement Ptolemy's regional maps in a manuscript of the *Geography* copied in 1427. He used the same method as Ptolemy, and the map is accompanied by a list of geographical coordinates of individual places; but his information was faulty and the resulting outline is barely recognisable. What are now the southern parts of Sweden are included in Denmark — 'Danorum Regio'.

Nancy, Bibliothèque Municipale

supplement the regional maps in the *Geography*. Some, both manuscript and printed, were included in copies of Ptolemy's work: a modern map to set beside the ancient one. Others were drawn for independent use. Most are of Italy, but alongside these we can place the two maps of Germany, one manuscript and one printed, attributed to Nicholas of Cusa, philosopher, cardinal and papal diplomat. The origins of both maps are mysterious; they were certainly produced long after Cusa's death in 1464 but may derive from a map he drew. Work on geography, geographical coordinates and maps would be in keeping with what we know of his scholarly interests and wide travels.

More immediately important for fifteenth-century maps than the work of theoretical geographers was the empirical knowledge gained by gradually lengthening voyages of discovery. Earlier travels had been slow to affect maps. Marco Polo's journeys in central Asia and China were made in the late thirteenth century, but the first map to incorporate their evidence was the Catalan atlas compiled in 1375; this is a large world map in folding form, drawn for the king of France. Again, assuming the Vinland map was drawn about 1440 and is not — as has been suggested — a modern forgery, its particular interest lies in the information it takes from the Icelandic sagas of the settlements in Greenland and Vinland, in North America (**44**). That these settlements took place is not in question, and the map adds nothing to our knowledge of them; its interest lies in showing that people in central Europe, where the map was seemingly drawn, were aware of them in the mid-fifteenth century. At the same time it cannot be claimed that the map offered up-to-date news of these western voyages, for they had been made more than four hundred years earlier.

The new discoveries made in the fifteenth century reached the maps much quicker. In the early years of portolan charts their coastlines of north-west Europe had been rapidly extended and corrected. By about 1330 Britain had changed from the rough rectangle of the *carte pisane* to more or less recognisable shape, Ireland had been added and the continental coast extended from Frisia beyond Jutland, with the Danish islands and Gotland making an appearance. But there the process had stopped. It had in fact gone as far as — indeed farther than — the needs of practical navigation demanded. The regular 'Flanders voyages' of Italian galleys had begun from Genoa in the late thirteenth century and from Venice in the early fourteenth; they went each year to ports on either side of the English Channel, but further north, in the North Sea and the Baltic, trade was in the hands of the Hansa merchants. Expansion — nautical and cartographical — continued, but in a different direction: south-west to the Atlantic islands and along the west coast of Africa.

The Canaries appear on a chart three years after their discovery in 1336,

44 The Vinland map

This world map first came to light, from an unknown source, a few years before it was published in 1965. It was then identified as having been drawn about 1440 in the area of the upper Rhine, perhaps at Basle. The outline of 'Vinlanda Insula' and the accompanying note (top left) aroused great interest, for they showed, what had hitherto been unsuspected, that the tenth-century Viking voyages to America were known in late-medieval central Europe. It was argued soon after, however, that the map is a modern forgery and the question remains unresolved.

New Haven, Yale University Library, MS. 350A

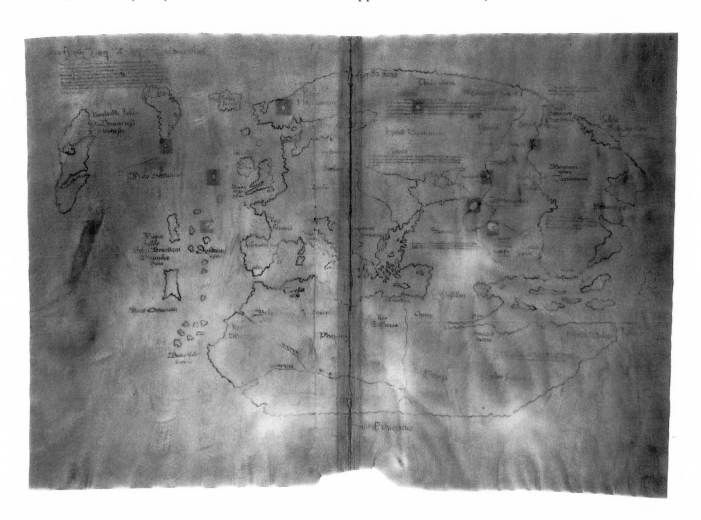

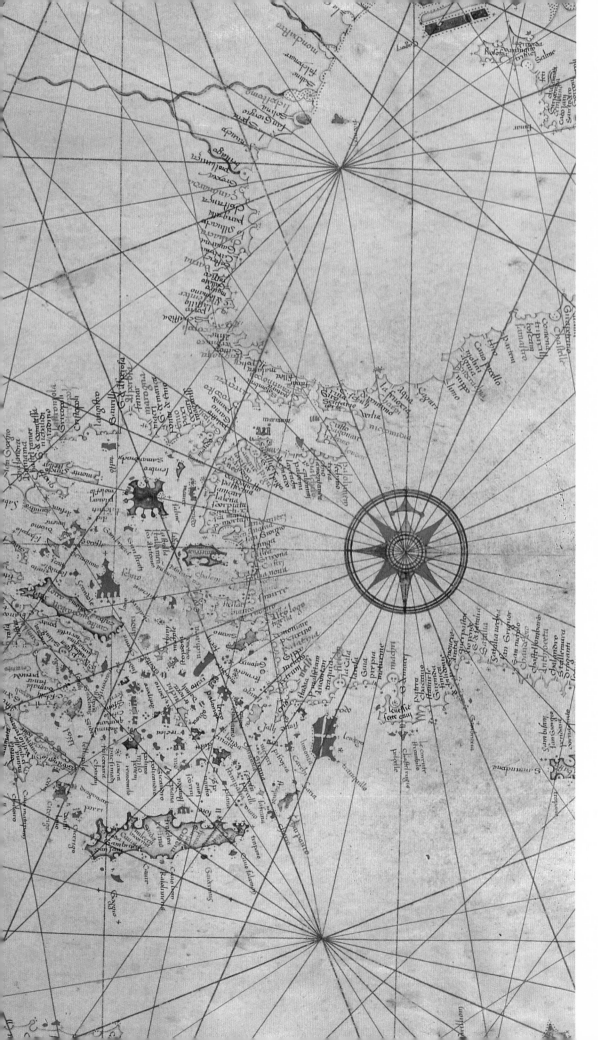

45 The Aegean on a portolan chart by Grazioso Benincasa
This map of the Aegean is from a chart drawn by Grazioso Benincasa at Ancona in 1470. It illustrates the detailed complexity of late portolan charts. Constantinople is in the centre, Crete at the foot and the intervening archipelago practically calls out for the fuller treatment provided by contemporary books of islands. The use of red to distinguish the more important place-names is a common feature on portolan charts.
British Library, Additional MS. 31318A

46 Chart of the Atlantic coastline by Grazioso Benincasa
In the fifteenth century portolan charts were often drawn in sections and bound to form a small atlas. This example, drawn by Grazioso Benincasa at Venice in 1469, contains six sheets, each measuring 41 by 33 centimetres. Comparison with Pietro Vesconte's chart of the same area (**31**) shows how little the map-maker's view of north-west Europe had changed over 150 years, reflecting the failure of Italian ships to extend their voyages beyond the English Channel.
British Library, Additional MS. 31315, ff.4v-5

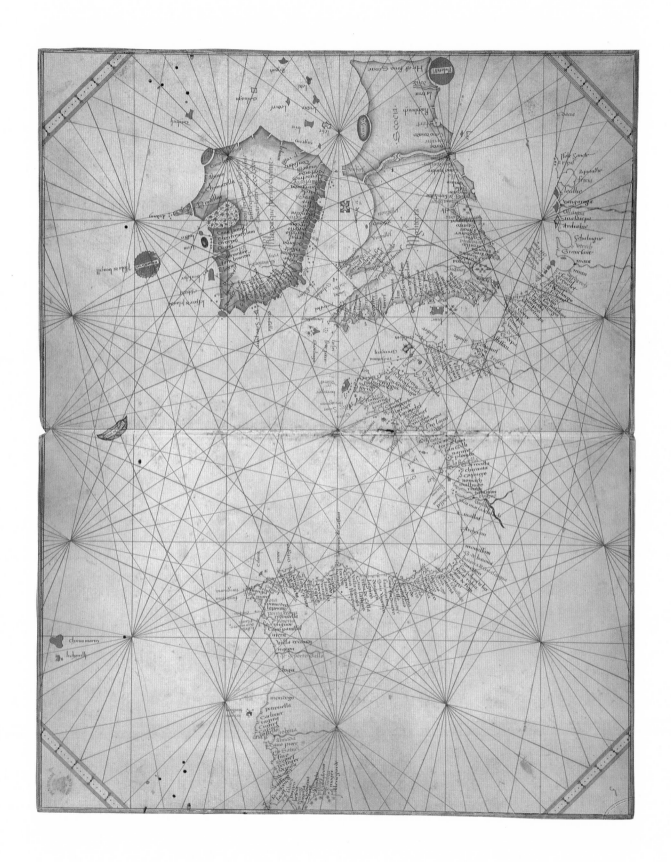

63

47-50 Four charts of the west
African coast by Grazioso
Benincasa

Successive atlases by Benincasa illustrate
the advance of voyages along the coast of
Africa and how chart-makers, after some
years' interval, incorporated the new
discoveries in their work. Luckily
Benincasa's charts usually include a note
saying when and where he drew them.

47 Dated 1463. The farthest points shown
are the Canary Islands and Cape Bojador.
British Library, Additional MS. 18454, ff.1v-2

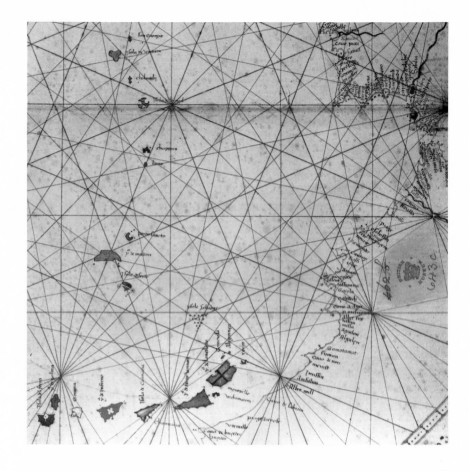

48 Dated 1468. Knowledge extends south
of the Tropic of Cancer as far as Cape
Blanc.
British Library, Additional MS. 6390, f.8

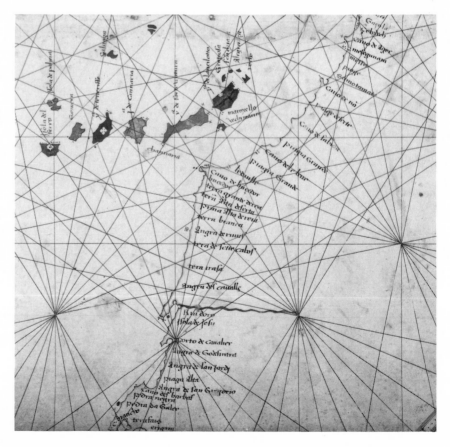

49 Dated 1467, but showing a position later than **48**. The coast is continued as far as Cape Verde; the river with two mouths is the Senegal.
British Library, Additional MS. 11547, f.6

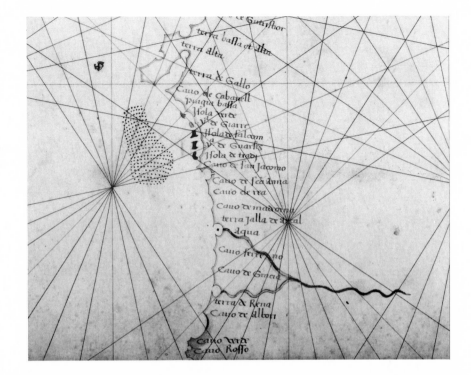

50 Dated 1473. The Cape Verde Islands have been added, and on the mainland the coastal outline has reached Sierra Leone.
British Library, Egerton MS. 2855, ff.6v-7

pages 66 and 67

51, 52 Charts of the Aegean from the Cornaro atlas

An atlas made for the Cornaro family of Venice at the end of the fifteenth century contains 35 portolan charts by various Venetian map-makers. In these two charts we can compare a single area as treated in two different workshops (**45**, the same area from Benincasa's chart of 1470, offers a further comparison). In general there is more variation in the outlines of the smaller islands than in the mainland coast, but there are some curious similarities — thus both maps outline Crete (bottom centre) in blue, Eubbea (left of centre) in red and, like many portolan charts, mark Rhodes (bottom right) with the cross, white on red, of the Hospitallers.

51 Copy of a chart by Nicolo Pasqualini, early fifteenth century.
British Library, Egerton MS. 73, opening 23

52 Chart by Benedetto Pesina, 1489.
British Library, Egerton MS. 73, opening 24

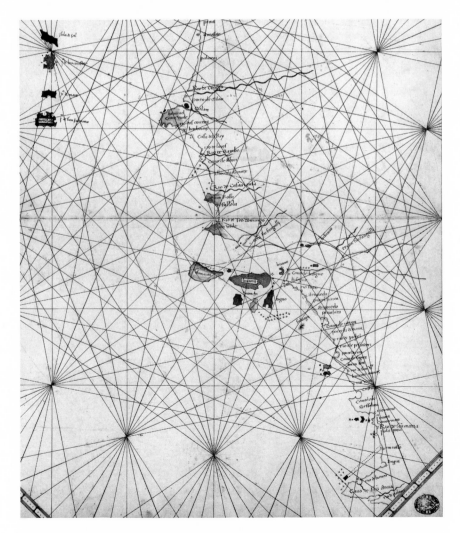

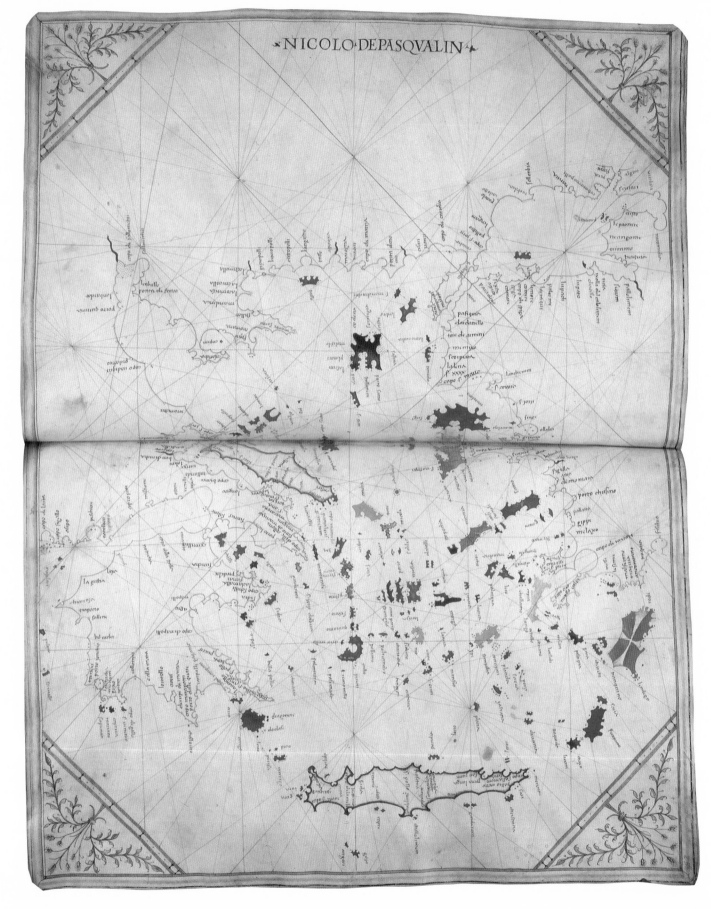

NICOLO·DEPASQVALIN

BENEDITVS · PE · SINA · FECIT ·
ANO DOMINI · M · CCCCLXXXVIIII ·
VENECIIS

but it is much harder to pinpoint the first mapping of the island groups discovered in the fifteenth century — Madeira, the Azores and the Cape Verde Islands. Legendary Atlantic islands, some with names later given to real ones, appear on portolan charts long before these groups are first known to have been visited. It is difficult to tell at what point reality overtook myth. On the other hand, successive advances along the African coast can be fairly easily followed on portolan charts and when, exceptionally, there is independent evidence of a chart's date there seems little time-lag between discovery and appearance on the map (**47-50**). Thus Cape Verde (by Dakar), reached by Dinis Dias in 1444, appears on a chart drawn in 1448 by Andrea Bianco; Bianco was an officer on a Venetian galley, and the chart was drawn at London, where a Flanders voyage must have taken him. However, it was the Portuguese who led the way in exploring the African coast, and they presumably recorded their discoveries on charts of their own — but these have not survived and the earliest known Portuguese portolan chart dates from the late fifteenth century. It is believed that knowledge of what was found on these voyages was in Portugal carefully guarded as a state secret, so these maps would not have been widely copied and recopied in the way that portolan charts were made in contemporary Italy and Spain.

It was not only on portolan charts that these new discoveries were

53 Africa and Europe on the Borgia world map

The Borgia world map is engraved on a circular iron plate, some 65 centimetres across. Its western (right-hand) half has Africa at the top with camels and black kings, and at the foot Scandinavia with a falcon and a man astride an elk. The shape of the Mediterranean owes little to portolan charts and the whole map recalls the thirteenth-century world maps. It in fact dates from the early or mid-fifteenth century.

Rome, Biblioteca Apostolica Vaticana, Borgiano XVI

recorded. The Cape of Good Hope, reached by Bartolomeo Dias in 1488, appears on the globe made in 1492 by Martin Behaim of Nuremberg and on the world maps that Henricus Martellus drew at Florence about the same time (**39**). In the thirteenth century England seems to have been the centre of production — or at least the source of inspiration — for the best world maps. For most of the fifteenth century it was Italy that held this position, but some of the products were little different in concept, style or content from those of England two hundred years earlier. The Borgia map, engraved on iron in the early or mid-fifteenth century and named from its later owner, presents a world outline scarcely more recognisable than the Hereford map, with a similar miscellany of information in the notes and pictures on the map surface (**53**). But in Fra Mauro's world map of 1459 we are in a new intellectual climate. Fra Mauro was a monk of Murano, near Venice, distinguished in his own time for his geographical work; his final achievement, produced with the help of Andrea Bianco, was a world map commissioned by the king of Portugal and now lost, but we have a contemporary copy that was made for the Venetian government (**54**). It is a large map, nearly 2 metres in diameter, and is covered with a mass of minute notes and other detail. But, though the change may be only in emphasis, geography has taken over. It is not just that we now have the more familiar European outline taken from the portolan charts and see the influence of the Ptolemy maps in other regions. The whole basis of the map, its raison d'être, is geographic. It is no longer a world diagram on which geographical information is simply one element among several others; it is, whatever its limitations, a map as we understand the word, in a way that the Ebstorf and Hereford maps are not.

Maps of regions

We have seen how in the early fourteenth century Pietro Vesconte used portolan charts as the basis for a map of Italy. Much earlier a few similarly ingenious persons may have elaborated some part of a world map to serve as a map of a single region. What seems to be the oldest map of this sort is of Asia, known only from a twelfth-century copy but perhaps compiled to illustrate works of Jerome in the fourth or fifth century (56). Again in the twelfth century one of the earliest manuscripts of Lambert of Saint-Omer's encyclopaedia contains not only the usual circular world map but also a quadrant-shaped map which is in fact the first map of Europe by itself that is known to us. It is not simply a section of Isidore of Seville's world map drawn large — it has been elaborated with detail drawn from other sources. Alternatively, it may be that these maps of Asia and Europe derive directly from older regional maps and that we should see them as relics of regional mapping in the Roman period.

However, the mid-thirteenth-century map of Britain by Matthew Paris certainly had a world map as its starting point. It survives in four versions, all in Matthew Paris's own hand (57, 58). They differ in detail, and one is markedly different from the others in general appearance, but they all represent an attempt — indeed, an extraordinarily successful attempt — to build up a map of Britain from its outline on a world map closely related to the Cotton map. As on the Cotton map there is a broad bay in the south-east corner of England, the Cornish peninsula is emphasised, the rest of the west coast of Britain is dominated by just two protrusions and two deep indentations, so that Galloway adjoins north Wales, and the north coast of Scotland sweeps in a gentle but indented curve from south-west to north-east. Some at least of the rivers may have come from the same source: they are sufficiently like the English rivers on the Hereford map to raise the possibility of a common origin. That Matthew Paris's maps derived from a map of the world is confirmed by the curved top left border of two of them, reflecting Britain's position at the edge of a curved world map, and by the notes or coastal outlines, also on two of the maps, of neighbouring lands — Britain is not viewed in isolation.

Within his outline Matthew Paris set quite a variety of features drawn from other sources. Central to all four maps is an itinerary, drawn as a straight line, from Newcastle to London and Dover, passing through St Albans, where he was himself a monk. Also included are some places within easy reach of St Albans and another group in north-east England around Tynemouth, where the abbey had a cell, as well as some prominent features whose existence must have been common knowledge — Hadrian's Wall, the Fenlands, the Forest of Dean. Besides these there are some more place-names and natural features, and some topographical notes such as 'A very cold area extending to the north', written on one of the maps in north-east Scotland. Like the authors of some world maps Matthew Paris realised how efficiently a map will convey any information relating to places.

55 Part of the map of Scotland by John Harding

John Harding's history of England down to the mid-fifteenth century was written primarily to demonstrate the English king's right to be overlord of Scotland, and three manuscripts of his work include a map. Here west is at the top and the River Forth, bridged at Stirling, all but cuts Scotland in two. The variety of walls and castles marking the towns is remarkable, but at Glasgow (top) and Dunfermline (centre) churches are drawn instead.

British Library, Lansdowne MS. 204, f.226v

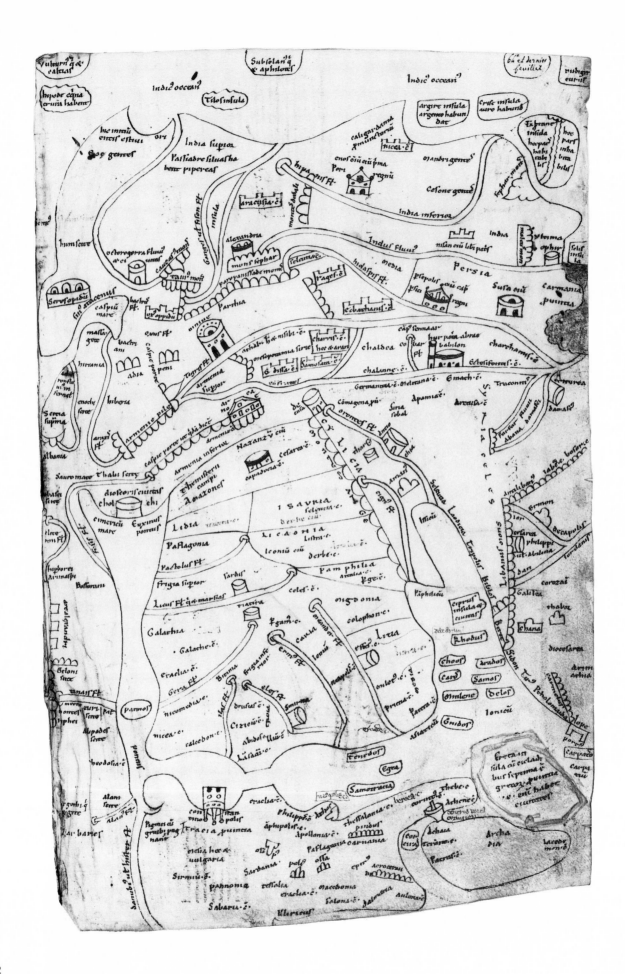

56 Jerome map of Asia

This map of Asia may have accompanied works of Jerome as early as the fourth or fifth century, but this twelfth-century copy is the only surviving example. East is at the top; at the bottom of the map are the Black Sea (left), Greece and the Aegean (centre) and the eastern Mediterranean (right). Damascus is shown (right centre) but Jerusalem and most of Palestine are beyond the right-hand edge of the map. The rows of semi-circles are mountains; many rivers are shown as though they are flowing out of conduits.

British Library, Additional MS. 10049, f.64

pages 74 and 75

57, 58 Maps of Britain by Matthew Paris

Four maps of Britain survive that were drawn by Matthew Paris in the mid-thirteenth century to accompany his chronicles; one of these two is the most fully worked of the four, the other the sketchiest. In outline and detail the two are more alike than a first glance might suggest. Both have the same vertical list of names forming an itinerary from Newcastle upon Tyne (**57**) or Pontefract ('pons fractus': **58**) to Dover, which is in the centre of the south coast.

57 The detail of the river system and the two walls across the country — Hadrian's Wall and presumably the Antonine Wall — are especially notable features.

British Library, Cotton MS. Claudius D.VI, f.12v

58 The inscription 'Britain, now called England' ('Britannia nunc dicta Anglia') may be a hint of the derivation of the map's outline from a world map of Roman origin.

British Library, Royal MS. 14 C.VII, f.5v

John Harding's mid-fifteenth-century map of Scotland is another British regional map with outline derived from world maps — it is clearly related to the outline of Scotland on Matthew Paris's maps and on the Hereford map (**55**). It too is known in several versions, illustrating different copies of his chronicle. Harding was an Englishman; as an 1819 British Museum catalogue put it, he was 'a restless and time-serving character', whose 'grand object was to stimulate, at all times, the princes whom he served to the conquest of Scotland'. Thus, unlike Matthew Paris's rather desolate picture of Scotland, he filled his outline with place-names and cities, giving a view of busy prosperity. This gives it particular interest as an early example of a map drawn for political purposes; but in the history of cartography it is much less important than the Gough map of Britain, which is perhaps a hundred years older, dating from the mid or late fourteenth century (**59, 61**).

Much of the Gough map's outline also stems from world maps, but the south and east coasts of England must have been taken from an up-to-date portolan chart. However, the map's interest lies in what it shows inland — not just one itinerary, like Matthew Paris's maps, but a whole network of roads, linking towns that are correctly placed on or between the branches of a quite elaborately drawn river system. On each section of road is a figure giving its length, but this is in local miles, a measure that varied from place to place. Viewed as a collection of itineraries it is extremely accurate, and places on different routes are mostly in a correct relationship to each other, but there seems to have been no attempt to maintain a consistent scale. Even so, the Gough map is an extraordinary production, hinting at cartographic principles then unknown outside the Mediterranean. It is the more extraordinary in that we know nothing of its origin or its use; its date is uncertain and we do not even know who owned it before 1768, when it belonged to the Suffolk antiquary Thomas Martin (Richard Gough, after whom it is named, bought it when Martin's collection was sold).

We know more about another group of regional maps that derived from portolan charts, those in the books of islands, or *isolarii*. These were travel books, giving interesting information — mythical, historical, geographical — about the islands of the eastern Mediterranean, and the account of each island was illustrated with a map. The earliest we know was written about 1420 by the Florentine Cristoforo Buondelmonti, who described his own journeys in a book addressed to his patron, Cardinal Giordano Orsini at Rome (**64, 65**). It seems to have initiated an entire genre: other *isolarii* were being written and copied or printed for another two hundred years. Certainly Buondelmonti's book was very popular and widely read, for it survives in many fifteenth-century manuscripts. Portolan charts probably provided the coastal outline for the maps in the book, but on all but the smallest islands internal features are shown, even in some detail — mountains, rivers and settlements, with thumbnail pictures of the principal buildings and towns. These were presumably the work of Buondelmonti himself, who must have sketched maps and pictures of the places he visited

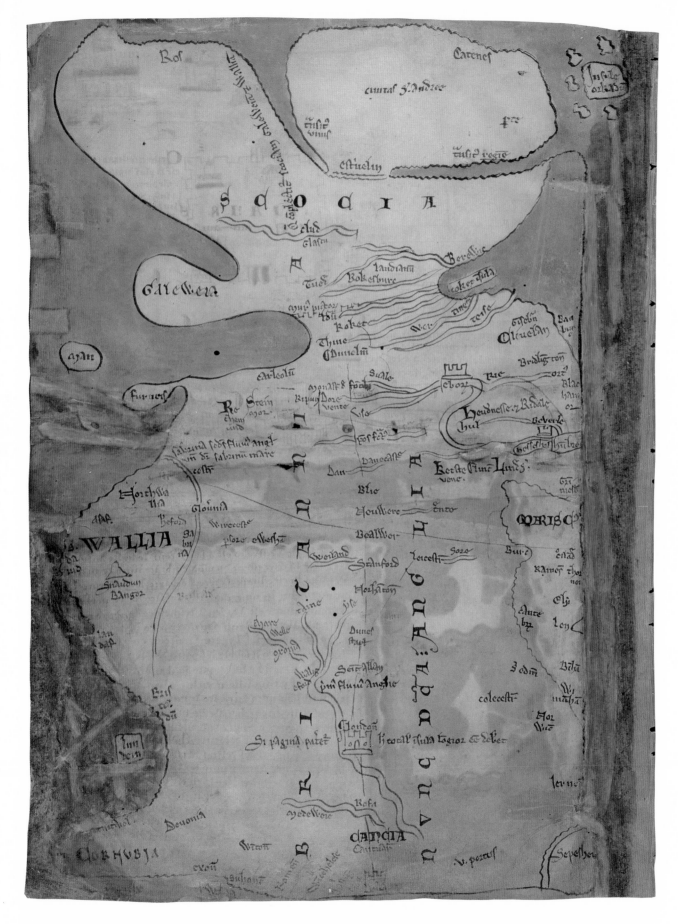

59 South-east
England on the
Gough map of
Britain

The Gough map's
outline of south-east
England derives from
contemporary
fourteenth-century
portolan charts. East
is at the top and
beyond the English
Channel Calais is
drawn as a walled
town. The thin lines
marking roads that
radiate from London
do not include one
through Kent to
Canterbury and
Dover, but a road
from Canterbury
follows the coast to
Lewes, Chichester
and Southampton.
Many rivers are
shown, and many
towns, not all of them
on rivers or roads.
Oxford, Bodleian Library,
MS. Gough Gen.Top. 1

In the fifteenth century several maps were drawn of the whole of Italy, by then the most map-conscious part of Europe. The outline and coastal detail were based on portolan charts, but inland features came from other sources, probably including contemporary regional maps from north Italy. On this example the area around Venice (bottom left) shows the map's great detail — towns, villages, and the elaborate river system. Like others, it is called a 'Modern map' of Italy, as though to supplement the ancient maps of Ptolemy, but being 1.5 metres long it can hardly have been meant to accompany them in an atlas.

British Library, Cotton Roll XIII.44

and described. In all they are an impressive achievement of regional cartography in the early fifteenth century.

We have seen that maps of Asia and Europe may have taken Roman regional maps rather than world maps as their starting point. The medieval maps that are most likely to stem directly from classical regional maps are those of Palestine, the Holy Land — indeed, this is one part of the Roman world from which a regional map actually survives in the Madaba mosaic (5). Medieval maps of Palestine are very varied, and we probably still have much to learn of how they are related to each other and to the mosaic or other maps of the Roman period that have now been lost. Some, of all types from the most diagrammatic to the most pictorial, show Jerusalem on a vastly larger scale than the rest of the country and one can see these either as regional maps or as plans of the city with the names and directions of other places simply as an adjunct. On the other hand, one of Matthew Paris's two maps of Palestine (this one exists in three versions) is dominated by its plan of Acre (73); when he drew it in the mid-thirteenth century this was the principal town still in the hands of the crusaders.

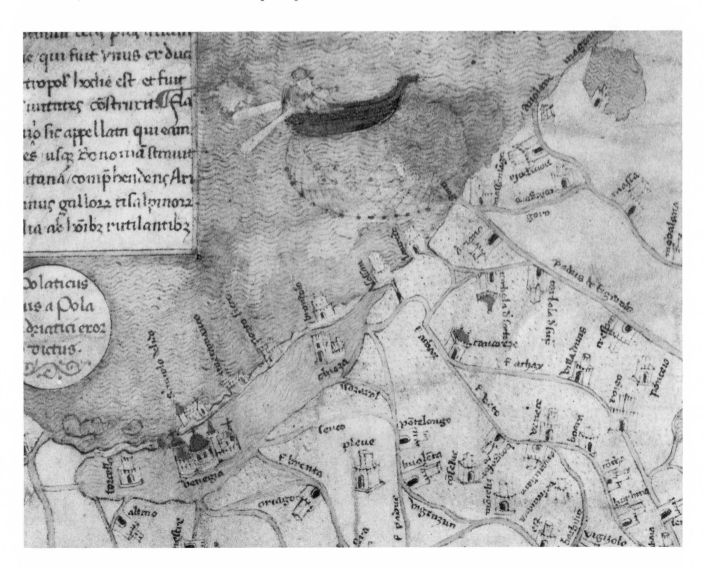

61 Gough map of Britain

The Gough map of Britain dates from about 1360. It measures 56 by 117 centimetres and has east at the top. The relatively accurate outline of the south-east coast derives from the most up-to-date portolan charts, but the rest of the outline comes from older sources. The map shows a network of roads, based primarily on London, naming towns and the distances between them. No similar medieval map of Britain or any other country is known, and how, why or by whom it was drawn is wholly mysterious.
Oxford, Bodleian Library, MS. Gough Gen. Top. 16

Detail: South-west England on the Gough Map
The Gough map's elongated south-western peninsula is related to Matthew Paris's maps (**57,58**) and the Cotton map (**19**). East is at the top and, on the curving line of the Severn, Bristol, Gloucester (both walled) and Worcester are all shown with churches with spires.
Oxford, Bodleian Library, MS. Gough Gen.Top.16

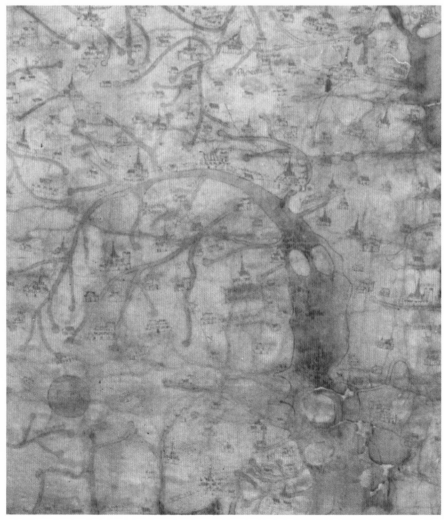

62 Map of Palestine by Pietro Vesconte

The text accompanying this map of Palestine, compiled by Pietro Vesconte about 1320, explains that each square of the grid measures one league or two miles; each town is then assigned to a particular square and it appears in the corresponding position on the map. East is at the top. The green at the bottom marks the Mediterranean, wrongly named the River Jordan ('Flumen Jordanus') by a much later annotator.

British Library, Additional MS. 27376*, ff.188v-189

The most interesting of the medieval maps of Palestine was drawn by Pietro Vesconte of Venice in about 1320 (62). In its purpose it was like Harding's map of Scotland: it illustrated a book by Marino Sanudo that urged a new crusade to reconquer the Holy Land, now entirely lost to the Christians. Cartographically, however, it was far more sophisticated than Harding's map, though more than a century older. It is covered with a network of squares, and the accompanying text explains that each represents one league or two miles; every town is placed in the appropriate square and — confirming the picture presented by the map — the text identifies the square where each town is to be found. The rivers and mountains were drawn in with less precision and they differ somewhat in the seven surviving copies of the book. This may seem to us an entirely normal and rational way to set out a map, but in the fourteenth century it represented an enormous conceptual leap, and confirms that Vesconte was a man of skill and imagination. Where he (or Sanudo) got the necessary information — the list locating the towns — we do not know; both this and the grid may derive from Arab sources, and a more remote connection with grid-based maps in China is not impossible.

However, some medieval regional maps owed nothing to classical models and drew neither their inspiration nor their coastal outlines from world maps or portolan charts. In north Italy a distinctive tradition of regional

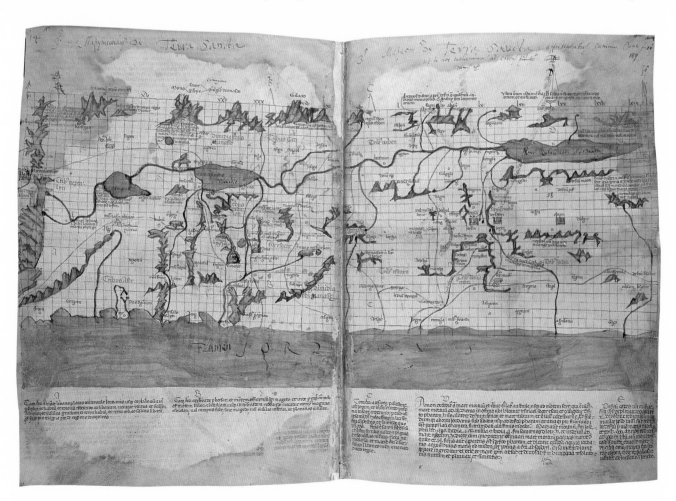

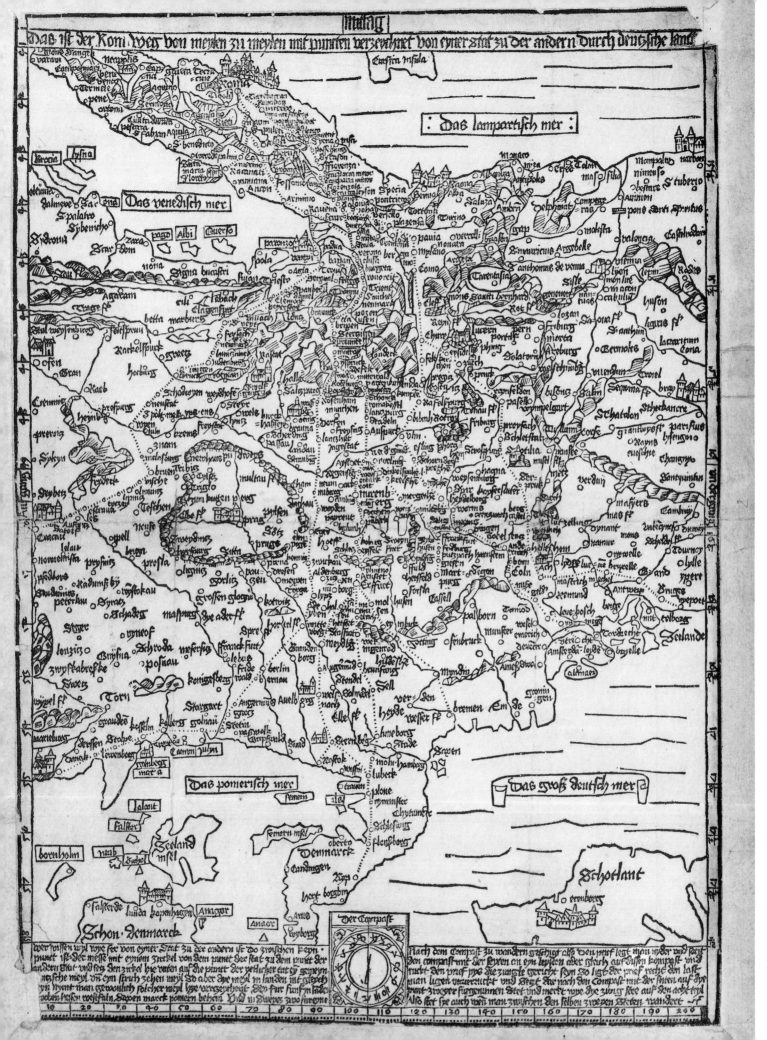

maps grew up in the later middle ages, a tradition that seems to have been independent of any outside source or precedent. Fourteen of these maps survive, and there are contemporary references to others that are now lost. The earliest dates from 1291, but most are of the fifteenth century. Some are of quite a small area, such as one of Lake Garda, some are of broader scope and two cover the whole of Lombardy. They are in varied styles; what was peculiar to north Italy was the idea of drawing regional maps of any sort, not a tradition of drawing them in a particular way. Several of the fifteenth-century maps are of areas centred on an important city — Brescia, Verona, Padua — drawn disproportionately large; often roads are prominently shown and distances given. Some of these may have been among the maps of Venetian territories that we know were drawn in the 1460s for the governing council at Venice, possibly Europe's first use of maps for administrative and military planning. They may well have contributed to our few fifteenth-century maps of the whole of Italy; on the largest of these there are many more internal features than on the maps in Paolino Veneto's work a century earlier, and it is in north Italy that most detail is shown (60).

Like these maps of Italy, the maps of Germany attributed to Nicholas of Cusa were — as we have seen — constructed in a framework of geographical coordinates. How these were calculated we do not know, nor how the detailed features were entered on the maps. It is much clearer what technique was used by Erhard Etzlaub of Nuremberg for his two printed maps that cover Germany and north Italy, one published probably in 1500 (63), the other in 1501: their internal detail seems to have come from careful measurement of many routes, their directions and distances. Roads on the maps are marked by series of dots, each corresponding to one German mile, and at the foot are instructions explaining how the map can be oriented by placing a compass on it. The compass was of course essential in constructing these maps, and it is significant that Etzlaub was himself a compass-maker. The use of the compass on land was spreading in the fifteenth century; a compass was, for instance, an essential component of the pocket sundials that seem to have come widely into use in this period.

In a sense these measured itinerary maps achieved on land what the portolan charts had achieved in maritime mapping two centuries earlier: every journey followed a route exactly drawn to scale. On land, where routes followed a limited number of roads, most travellers' needs would be adequately met by a written itinerary or by a simple itinerary map, with distances entered but not drawn to scale, such as the Gough map or some of the fifteenth-century maps from north Italy. Drawing the itineraries to scale was of course an improvement, enabling distances to be assessed along routes unpredicted by the map-maker, but this need not have been seen as essential to a good road map. At sea, on the other hand, where a ship might follow any of an infinite number of routes, the map would have to be drawn to scale if it was to offer any real guidance at all on distances. It is not surprising that sea charts were drawn to scale so much earlier than land maps.

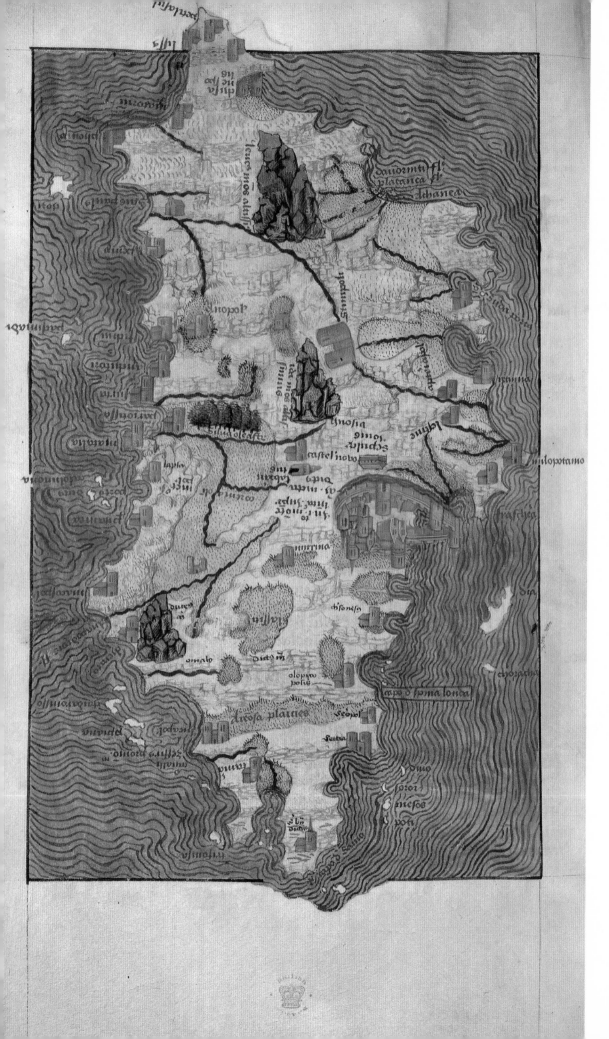

64, 65 Maps from the book of islands by Cristoforo Buondelmonti

Cristoforo Buondelmonti's book of islands, written about 1420, was a popular work, a travelogue of the islands of the eastern Mediterranean. The account of each island was accompanied by a map, the whole forming effectively a regional atlas, something hitherto unknown in medieval Europe. These two pages are from a manuscript copied in 1485.

64 The map of Crete has west at the top. Although it is a page in a book it follows the convention of some contemporary loose maps — many of its pictures and names are meant to be viewed with the map upside down or even sideways.
British Library, Arundel MS. 93, f.134v

65 The plan of Constantinople and Pera, with north at the top, betrays the book's Italian origin, for its style and conventions are the same as some medieval plans of Italian cities.
British Library, Arundel MS. 93, f.155

PERA

pera

CONSTAN=
TINOPOLIS.

ciuitas

ntuio
ciuitas

palaü Imp᷑nis

porta

porta de lucto

Sas de mer᷑

Sas geor
hmo

Turquia

chiramo

portus olim
palaci im
peratoris

Scutari

Calchedona

palangu

portus sed destruit
precepto teutorum

66 Anonymous map of the Nuremberg region

This map, printed from a wood-block in the early sixteenth century, is similar to Erhard Etzlaub's map of 1492: a circle centred on Nuremberg, with roads shown by dotted lines, one dot for every German mile. Unlike Etzlaub's map north, not south, is at the top. The wavy line across the upper part of the map is the river Main; the hills on the right ('Behemer Walt') are the Bohemian Forest.
British Library, Maps C.7.b.18

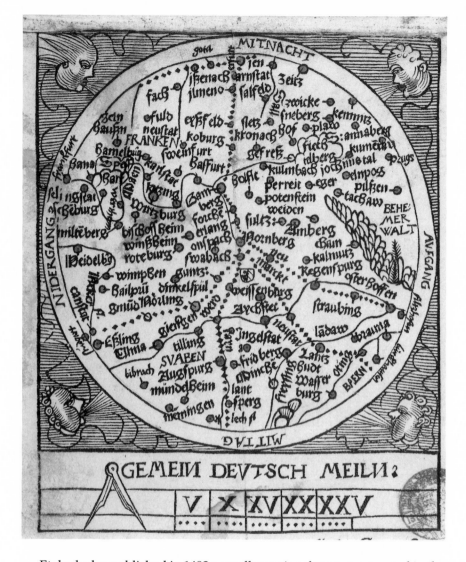

67 Panoramic map of east Germany

Book of the four loves by Konrad Celtes, published at Nuremberg in 1502, includes a panoramic map of each of the four quarters of Germany. The east quarter has the Carpathians at the bottom, and the Vistula flows past a city that is probably Cracow, mentioned in the scroll above, to a scene of people bathing and dancing on its bank. Despite the map's pictorial form it pays lip service to the scale-maps of Etzlaub in the scale of distances along three of its sides.
British Library, C.57.g.11, f.[8]v

Etzlaub also published in 1492 a smaller regional map constructed in the same way as his maps of Germany with north Italy; it took the form of a circle, centred on Nuremberg, with a radius of sixteen German miles (**66**). South Germany was one area that led the way in the growing understanding of cartography, so that in the course of the next century knowledge and use of maps had spread throughout Europe. But it was at quite a late stage in this process that scale-maps like Etzlaub's would be widely understood and used. They were among the most sophisticated maps of their time, and contemporaries may well have found it easier to understand the strange panoramic maps of the four quarters of Germany that were published in 1502, also at Nuremberg, in a book by Konrad Celtes, humanist scholar and Germany's first poet laureate (**67**). When we look at local maps we see still more clearly how the idea of drawing maps spread only slowly and was grasped with difficulty in late medieval Europe.

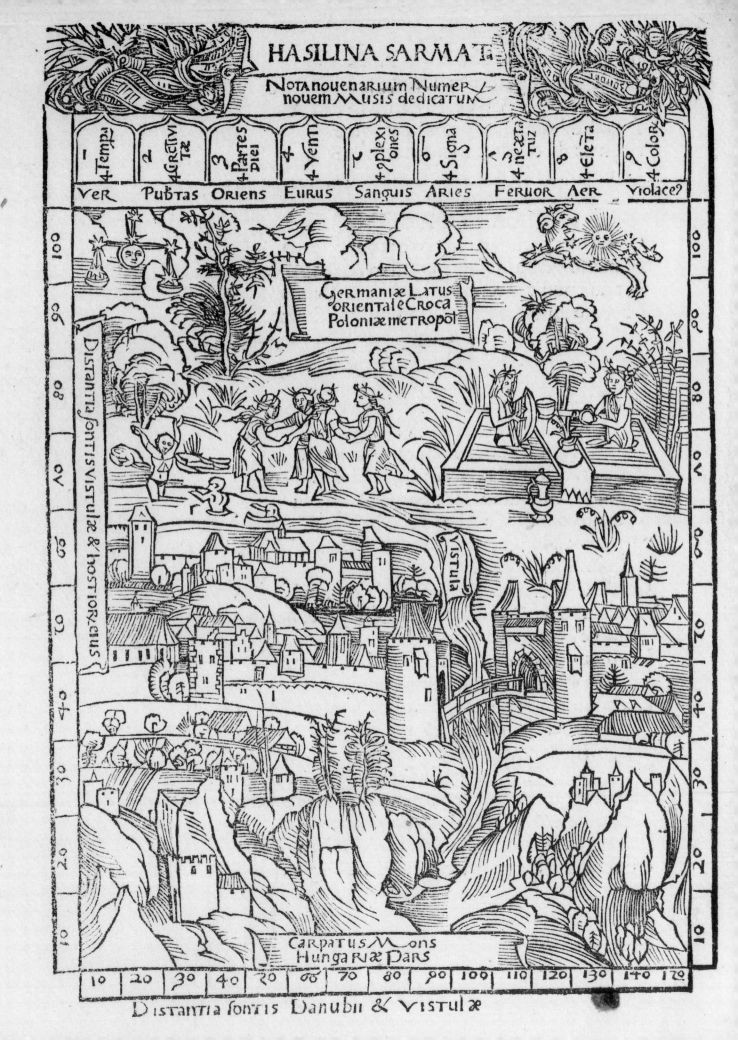

CHAPTER SIX

Local maps

BESIDES the maps of Palestine many of the plans of Jerusalem drawn in the middle ages probably derive from those of the Roman period. Most medieval plans of Jerusalem are more diagrammatic than realistic, for they show the city within circular walls, its shape neither in the middle ages nor in antiquity (71). These maps may be related to the representation of Jerusalem on the Madaba mosaic. But already in the twelfth century, when the city was in the hands of the crusaders, we find a map of its principal streets and monuments set more realistically in a parallelogram, and in the early fourteenth century Pietro Vesconte produced a plan of Jerusalem that was closely based on direct observation (72). He also produced plans of Antioch and Acre — but in this last he had been anticipated by the vastly disproportionate plan of Acre on Matthew Paris's map of Palestine (73). The source of Matthew Paris's map is not known; with the camel beside it, it is oddly reminiscent of the stylised Jerusalem on the Ebstorf map. In the fourteenth and fifteenth centuries several plans of Jerusalem resulted from pilgrims' visits, culminating in the magnificent bird's-eye view that appears in — indeed, again it wholly dominates — the woodcut map of Palestine accompanying Bernhard von Breydenbach's account of his visit to the Holy Land (69). This was published in 1486; the view was the work of Erhard Reuwich, an artist from Utrecht whom Breydenbach, himself a canon of Mainz, took with him to record the journey in pictures.

This illustrates one important point about medieval local maps, maps of areas personally known to their compilers. What we see are not simple ground plans — detailed features above ground level were drawn pictorially, like the towns on most other medieval maps. These pictures might be realistic or conventional; but it means that we have to see as a map any representation of landscape viewed as though from above the ground, from some point unattainable in reality. It means too that these picture-maps of the middle ages were the ancestors of both the large-scale maps and the bird's-eye views of later ages. It is only in work of the sixteenth century, when consistent scale began to be applied to local mapping, that it becomes possible to draw a distinction between the two ways of depicting landscape.

We see this in city plans from medieval Italy. These owe nothing to classical models; the earliest we know, of Verona in the tenth century and Rome in the twelfth, seem entirely original works. Each is a more or less symbolic representation — pictures of some of the city's more distinctive monuments within conventional walls, akin to the little pictures of London and other towns on Matthew Paris's itinerary(1). But from this beginning pictorial plans of cities were drawn with ever increasing detail and realism. They are not numerous; Rome has the largest number, and these are based on only half a dozen prototypes. But they include Florence, Milan and several towns outside Italy in the eastern Mediterranean — the plan of Constantinople in Buondelmonti's book of islands belongs to this group (65). The tradition culminated in the late fifteenth century with some wholly

68 Map of Inclesmoor in Yorkshire
This is a slightly later copy of a map drawn about 1407 in connection with a law-suit over rights of pasture and peat-cutting in Inclesmoor, an area south-east of Goole. South is at the top; on the left are the rivers Trent and (in its former course) Don. In its careful drawings of villages, bridges, wayside crosses, meadow plants and much else besides, the map presents an extraordinarily detailed picture of late-medieval landscape.
London, Public Record Office, MPC 56

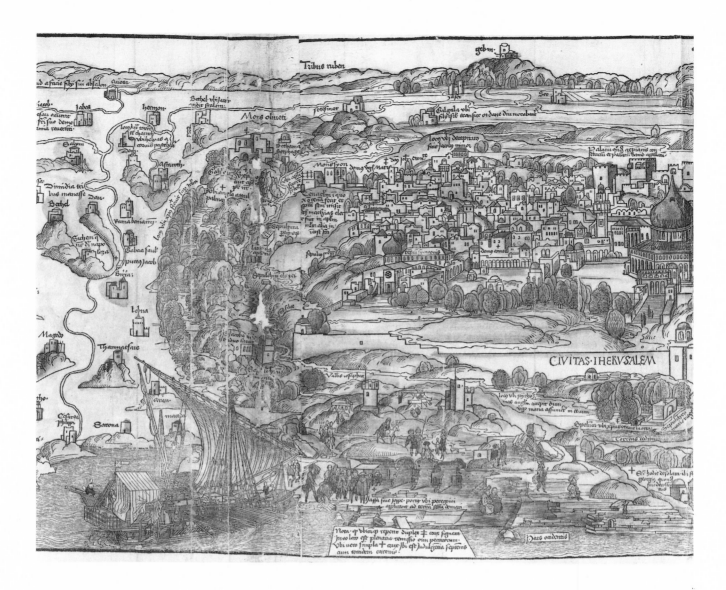

69 Part of Bernhard von Breydenbach's map of Palestine

Bernhard von Breydenbach's account of his visit to the Holy Land was published in 1486. Among its woodcut illustrations is a map of Palestine, dominated by a panoramic view of Jerusalem. East is at the top of the map, so the Mediterranean coast is at the foot. But Jerusalem is drawn as though looking westward, with its eastern wall in the foreground. It is thus misplaced in relation to its surroundings and Mount Sion and the Mount of Olives ('Mons syon', 'Mons oliueti'), shown close together (top centre) are really on opposite sides of the city.

British Library, C.20.e.3

realistic and very detailed bird's-eye views of which the finest is undoubtedly the view of Venice by Jacopo de' Barbari, printed from wood-blocks in 1500 (**70**).

An earlier plan of Venice, drawn in the twelfth century but known only from later copies, is a true ground-plan, drawn more or less to scale. This, with some other indications, raises the interesting possibility that measured scale-plans, though clearly very rare, were not unknown in the towns of medieval Italy. But the only surviving medieval city plan that is specifically drawn to scale — it even has a scale-bar — is of Vienna, with a smaller inset plan of Bratislava (**74**). We know nothing of how, why or by whom it was drawn, but it dates from about 1422; we may guess at Italian influence or even that it owed something to the geographic work then proceeding at Vienna and Klosterneuburg.

The origin of the plan of Vienna is scarcely more mysterious than the distribution of other local maps and plans in medieval Europe. Even when we count every possible map — the few lines roughly sketched with a couple of place-names, the outline plan of a building, the diagram of part

70 Panorama of Venice by Jacopo de' Barbari

The culmination of bird's-eye views of medieval Italian cities, Jacopo de' Barbari's magnificent panorama of Venice was printed in 1500 from six wood-blocks; it measures 1.3 by 2.8 metres. It was probably constructed from many drawings made from high buildings — its detail and general accuracy are extraordinary. In a view like this the image of the city served as a statement of its power and prestige; it was more than simply functional or even decorative in intent. It was only in the sixteenth century that local maps and bird's-eye views began to follow separate paths — medieval picture-maps were the ancestors of both.
London, British Museum

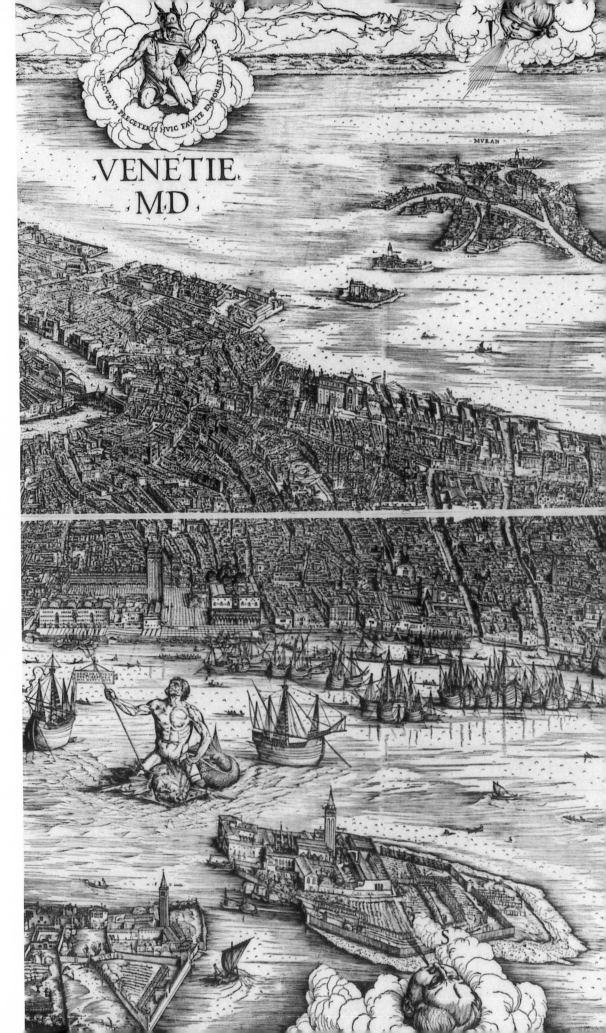

VENETIE M·D

MVRAN

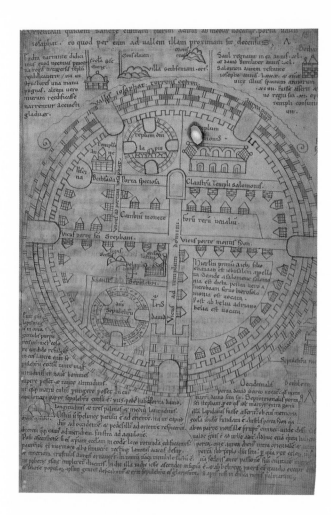

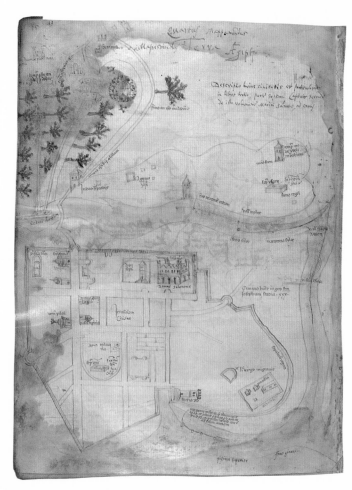

71 Circular plan of Jerusalem

Most medieval plans of Jerusalem give it circular walls (it was actually four-sided) and were probably of classical origin — compare its oval form on the Madaba mosaic (**5**). This thirteenth-century example shows some streets and monuments, among them the Holy Sepulchre (bottom left) and the Temple of Solomon (top right). Outside the walls at the top a wavy line marks the Valley of Jehoshaphat and the River Cedron, and among the features beyond is the Mount of Olives.
British Library, Additional MS. 32343, f.15v

72 Plan of Jerusalem by Pietro Vesconte

Pietro Vesconte's plan of Jerusalem, which dates from about 1320, was closer to reality than the more usual medieval circular plans of the city. The general shape of the walls and of the street pattern is fairly correct. It is not, however, drawn to scale and there is no sign that measurement on the ground played any part in its construction. East is at the top and the map extends in this direction as far as Bethany ('Betania').
British Library, Additional MS. 27376*, f.189v

right

73 Map of Palestine by Matthew Paris

This map of Palestine that Matthew Paris drew in mid-thirteenth-century England is dominated by its plan of Acre, the large walled enclosure with a camel outside it. Jerusalem, another walled enclosure (top right) is small by comparison, and other coastal cities (centre right) are marked simply by castles and towers. It is not known where Matthew Paris got his information about Acre, which a Latin note on the map describes as 'the hope and refuge of all Christians in the Holy Land' — it was the last surviving foothold of the crusaders there.
British Library, Royal MS. 14 C.VII, ff.4v-5

of an estate — very few exist from the fifteenth century and very few indeed before 1400. From England some 35 in all are known, more than from any comparable area, starting with the mid-twelfth-century plan of Canterbury Cathedral; they are distributed fairly evenly over the country, with some concentration in eastern England around the Wash (68, 75, 76). From Ireland, however, we have only a supposed seating plan of the Hall of Tara, and from Wales and Scotland nothing at all. From the Netherlands there are some fifteen plans from 1307 onwards, all from a fairly narrow coastal strip stretching from Hilversum to Bruges, but moving further east there is practically nothing — from the whole of Scandinavia, Poland and north Germany we have only two sketch maps of about 1464 showing lands of the Teutonic Order in Pomerania. Apart from the city plans and the group of regional maps from north Italy there are probably very few Italian local maps; in France the position is less clear, but about a dozen are recorded, all from the east and south (77), and it is possible that from Spain and Portugal there are none at all.

New discoveries may modify this strange pattern of distribution, but are unlikely to change it radically. It is the more strange, in that the local maps in any particular area, such as England or the Netherlands, conform to no particular form or style; they are an extraordinary mixture, from the careful

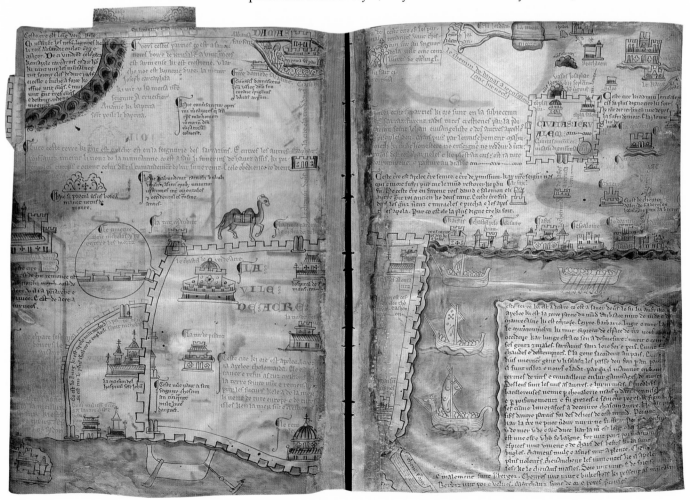

74 Plans of Vienna and Bratislava

A mid-fifteenth-century copy of a plan of Vienna drawn about 1422, this is the earliest medieval local map to be explicitly to scale. The plan of Bratislava appears as an inset (top left) with a view of its castle. The author of the map is not known, nor how the idea arose of drawing it to scale.
Vienna, Historisches Museum der Stadt Wien, I.N. 31.018

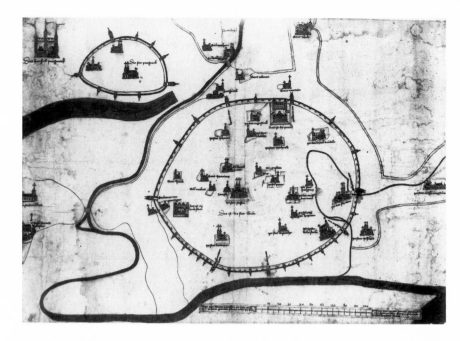

bird's-eye view to the roughly sketched ground-plan. Just as we saw in the regional maps from north Italy, the crucial point was simply the idea of drawing maps, not drawing them in some particular way. We may reasonably ask what it was that led people in these areas occasionally to draw these local maps, but we can only guess the answer. The cause may well have differed from one area to another. Certainly in France, probably also in the Netherlands and Italy, local maps were drawn to produce in courts of law as illustrative evidence of rights and claims, following the precepts of the Italian legal writer, Bartolo da Sassoferrato; given this impetus, they will sometimes have been drawn for other purposes as well. But there is nothing to suggest that maps were used before the sixteenth century in law-courts in England. Here the modest growth of local map-making from the late fourteenth century onwards may be connected with the way English builders now began to produce plans of new buildings to show their clients; these plans are mentioned in contracts, though only a single example survives. From southern Germany and central Europe on the other hand we have a considerable number of late-medieval building plans, drawn with great care and — unlike the solitary English one — to scale. They may lie behind the 1422 plan of Vienna and Bratislava, but apart from a diagram of 1441 showing an estate on the Rhine, near Strasbourg, no other local map is known from this area until the very end of the fifteenth century. Unlike the English building plans, however, they were drawn not to show clients but as a working tool, a technique of the builders' craft, and may have been carefully guarded as a trade secret.

The one question we need not ask is why there were so few local plans in the middle ages and none at all over much of Europe. Having now looked at every kind of medieval map we might conclude that Italy and England were more map-minded than any other parts of the continent, that someone living in the later middle ages would be more likely to come across a map

75 Plan of Clenchwarton in Norfolk

People in the middle ages hardly ever drew even so simple a sketch-map as this. Drawn on a flyleaf of a cartulary of Blackborough Priory, it measures about 15 by 14 centimetres and shows part of the village of Clenchwarton, Norfolk. At the top is the church, with crudely drawn steeple; at the bottom an oval feature in a yard is identified as a 'Welle'.

British Library, Egerton MS. 3137, f.1v

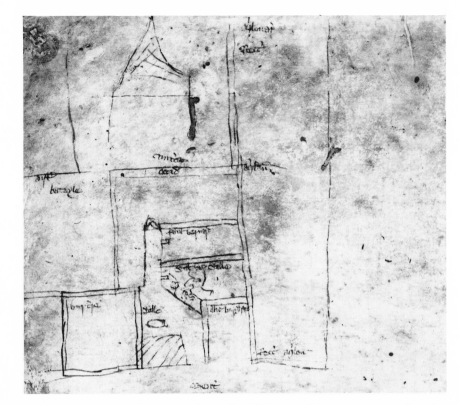

in these two areas than anywhere else. But even here maps were few in number and largely restricted to particular uses by limited groups of people. And of all the aspects of medieval mapping we have seen, it is the distribution of local maps that brings home most clearly the truth of our opening sentence. Maps were practically unknown in the middle ages.

FURTHER READING

For further reading on medieval maps consult the comprehensive account in *The History of Cartography*, edited by J.B. Harley and David Woodward, vol. 1 (Chicago and London, The University of Chicago Press, 1987), pp.283-500, and the works cited there. Important later work includes T. Campbell, *The Earliest Printed Maps 1472-1500* (London, British Library, 1987), and several articles on medieval maps, in English and French, in *Géographie du monde au moyen âge et à la renaissance*, ed. M. Pelletier (Paris, Comité des Travaux Historiques et Scientifiques, 1989). An earlier general discussion of medieval maps is in L. Bagrow, *History of Cartography*, ed. R.A. Skelton (London, C.A. Watts, 1964; enlarged edition, Chicago, Precedent Publishing, 1985). Among more specialised works, with further illustrations, are C.R. Beazley, *The Dawn of Modern Geography* (London, J. Murray, 3v., 1897-1906), which covers the period before the tenth century; M. Destombes, *Mappemondes AD 1200-1500* (Amsterdam, N. Israel, 1964), a detailed catalogue of world maps; and P.D.A. Harvey, *The History of Topographical Maps* (London, Thames and Hudson, 1980), which deals with regional and local mapping.

76 Plan of springs at Wormley in Hertfordshire
This plan of the springs at Wormley, Hertfordshire, from which Waltham Abbey drew its water, was copied in the mid-thirteenth century from an original drawn in the 1220s. It illustrates an account of how the three-mile long pipe was laid to the abbey. At the top is the road to Cheshunt; the three circles are the springs from which the water passed through two tanks before entering the pipe. On the cross at the top the splayed foot marks the east, the earliest known direction pointer on a medieval map.
British Library, Harley MS. 391, f.6

77 Plan of villages in the Côte-d'Or
As reproduced here this plan has east at the top, looking across the River Saône, but like many medieval maps it is made to be seen from several directions — there is no 'right way up'. Measuring 62 by 56 centimetres it was produced in 1460 to show the boundary between the kingdom of France and the duchy of Burgundy where it passed through the fields between three villages.
Dijon, Archives Départementales de la Côte-d'Or, B.263

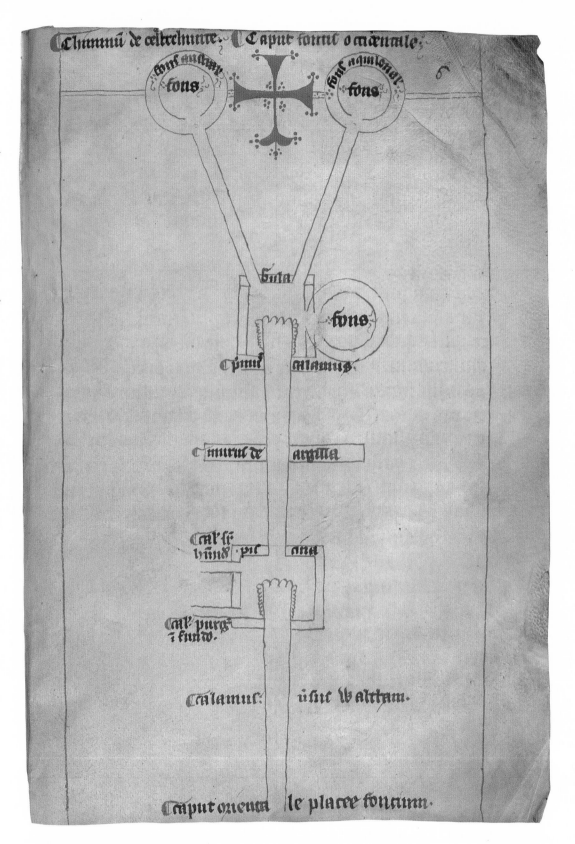